Katie Luther,
FIRST LADY OF THE
REFORMATION

OTHER BOOKS BY RUTH A. TUCKER

Katie Luther,
FIRST LADY OF THE
REFORMATION

The Unconventional Life of Katharina von Bora

RUTH A. TUCKER

ZONDERVAN

Katie Luther, First Lady of the Reformation
Copyright © 2017 by Ruth A. Tucker

This title is also available as a Zondervan ebook.

Requests for information should be addressed to:
Zondervan, *3900 Sparks Dr. SE, Grand Rapids, Michigan 49546*

ISBN 978-0-310-53215-6 (softcover)

Cover design: Darren Welch
Cover image: Private Collection Photo © Christie's Images/Bridgeman Images
Interior design: Kait Lamphere

Printed in the United States of America

17 18 19 20 21 22 23 24 25 26 27 /DCI/ 15 14 13 12 11 10 9 8 7 6 5 4 3 2

Contents

Introduction

KATHARINA VON BORA
FOR ALL SEASONS

Katharina von Bora. Tall, slender, dark-haired, piercing eyes, passionate voice, stomping her foot in defiance, refusing to be intimidated. She was headstrong and determined. No shrinking, submissive, subdued, sweet lady was she. She knew what she wanted, and not even Martin Luther could stop her. The crowd was riveted to her every word, clucking, cheering, laughing, and clapping. I close my eyes and can still hear her distinct Kenyan-British accent.

She had begged for the role. It was the class play for our final session of my church history course at Moffat Bible College in Kijabe, Kenya. The previous year we had burned Polycarp at the stake—almost literally, when his shabby, black choir robe caught fire. He was tackled by fellow students, who quickly put out the flames, and the drama continued as though the football pile-up had been planned. The whole student body, faculty, and staff had come out for the performance, and there was great anticipation this year. Word-of-mouth publicity had done its trick—much buzz about Martin Luther and Katie, starring Kotut and Beatrice.

As a class we had chosen the topic. Parts were assigned—or rather fought over, with the loudest and most articulate students snatching lead roles. Indeed, voice projection was critical. If you were loud, you were in. I was the director, no challenge on that, working with the

7

students on choreography and chronological events. From there, they created the dialogue, with my insistence that they keep things snappy. No long speeches. They were ready and a tad nervous on that cool, sunny morning. The crowd was bigger than the previous year, now joined by students from the nearby nursing school. I stood backstage behind a small curtain crowded with actors, ready to push a Tetzel or Pope Leo X onto the "stage" if they didn't hear their cue.

Curbing his usual class-clown tendencies, Kennedy welcomed the noisy crowd and presented appropriate background information. There was a momentary hush. Then, wearing Polycarp's shabby, now singed, black robe, Martin strutted out from behind the curtain onto the grassy knoll, carrying on like a good sixteenth-century Reformer: hammering theses to a door, railing against indulgences, preaching salvation by faith, and doing what my students loved most, building a fire—in this case to burn a papal bull.

But it was Katie who stole the show. She entered Wittenberg in a wagon with my two other female students and several males dressed in drag—the best we could do for nuns' attire. Martin quickly finds husbands for them, all except for Katie. Having been stood up by the man she thought was her fiancé, she is already vulnerable, and now she alone is left. Martin seeks out a worthy gentleman, whom Katie agrees to marry (or, as she emphasizes, Martin himself), but the man is threatened by this sassy, assertive woman.

Poor Martin. A confirmed bachelor himself, he has been assigned to find husbands for them all. So, with no other prospects, he brings out Casper Glatz. No! It can't be. Casper Glatz? The students had unanimously picked our oldest white missionary professor for the part. He was perfect: short, bald, self-conscious, clueless. The haughty Katie sizes him up and shreds him right there in front of everyone. No way will she ever marry Casper. The audience howled with laughter. I have no recollection of exactly where we went with the drama from there, but it was truly a smash hit, curtain calls to prove it.

Katharina, wife of Martin Luther, was by any measure the First Lady of the Reformation. Important as she was, however, she would remain unknown to us were it not for her larger-than-life husband. Yet she stands alone in her own right, albeit as a woman: first lady, second sex.

Second sex. Martin was first and Katie second. According to the creation account, Aristotle, the apostle Paul, Augustine, Aquinas, and Luther himself, man was first, woman second. And still today, whether in Kenya or the United States Senate. No one need read Simone de Beauvoir's *Second Sex* to know that much. But before we even have time to formulate our lament for such discrimination, a biblical Sarah or Rebekah pops out of the pages. Or a Cleopatra or Katie von Bora. Sassy, spirited, and sometimes laughing aloud at that bumbling first sex. Sure, Adam was first. But was he really? Just ask Eve. Ask Katie.

For me, making Katharina von Bora relevant to my Kenyan students was relatively easy. They were very familiar with the problems related to arranged marriages and extended families all living under one roof. They had grown up in homes without modern conveniences, running water, or electricity. They understood the backbreaking toil of farmwork on their family *shambas*. They knew what it was like to carry heavy loads of wood to cook the next meal. They all had a *cho* out back with no toilet paper, and they were all too familiar with the bloody rags women used during their monthly periods. Emergency rooms and good doctors were too often a tragic death away. Childbirth was perilous. Hunger was real. Indeed, times were tough for my Kenyan students. They identified with daily life in Wittenberg five hundred years ago. And like the folks around town back then, they could name women just like Katie—women who were not afraid to speak up in male-dominated marriages and communities. Indeed, I have no doubt they understood the women, customs, and culture of that era far better than I did.

So how do we make a five-hundred-year-old Katharina relevant to North American culture? Is there anything she has to say to Western women and men today? Why should we take the time to make her acquaintance?

In many ways, Katharina's voice echoes among modern women, wives, and mothers who have carved out careers of their own. And unlike so many of the Reformation women we read about, her primary vocation was not related to ministry. She was a farmer and a brewer with a boarding house the size of a Holiday Inn. All that with a large family and nursing responsibilities. In many ways, Katie could walk right into the twenty-first century—and claim *lean in* as her motto.

Here we focus our sights on her, while at the same time bringing to the fore her predecessors and contemporaries, both Reformed and Catholic. What was it like for a young woman to grow up in a convent? Were they the fortunate girls of the day, or were they pitiful cast-offs, incarcerated in cells? What were their hopes and fears? Does the story of Williswind shed light on convent life? She was a little-known eighth-century nun who suffered dreadful aftereffects of what was most likely rape at the hands of violent backwoods thugs.[1] Had Katharina heard such stories? Did she fear the all-too-real monsters breaking down the monastery walls?

Many of Katharina's predecessors in monasticism are familiar names like Clare of Assisi and Hildegard of Bingen. Others are new to us, but what can we learn about the nun Katharina from their experiences and from the nuns of her own day—some who escaped, others who chose to remain in convents? And what about Reformed women of the era? Do the lives of Katherine Zell, Argula von Grumbach, Renee of Fererra, and others shed light on Katharina? They do. But Katharina stands alone, even as she speaks for all of us in every age and culture.

Indeed, she is a woman for all seasons. More than that, her life embodies all that is human—struggles and sorrows and joys that belong to every culture and all generations: her second-guessing difficult decisions, a hectic schedule, sleepless nights, family illness and mental health issues, deaths of children. These are not gender-related troubles. Nor is her lost love and loneliness as a single or her marital clashes related to money or personality differences. These are human problems. That is not to deny, however, that many troubling matters for her were related to gender and culture. She carried women's burdens that no man can fully comprehend—burdens we shall encounter as we glimpse her life from childhood to old age.

But most striking is her singularity—her thoroughly unconventional life. She is not easily lost in the crowd of history, even considering the paucity of original sources. She cannot be straitjacketed into the role of a proper Reformation wife—a wife acceptable neither for the sixteenth century nor for today. That she was an assertive and decisive manager of household and business affairs has been well documented, and today we praise her for that. Less, however, has been sorted out regarding her religious role—or lack thereof—as we shall see.

It is critical that we do not mold Katie into a modern-day evangelical. Martin more easily serves such a purpose in that he was adept at God-talk, emphasized salvation by faith alone, and testified to being born again. Not so Katie. Not, if we were to use the definition of a true Christian as opposed to a "nominal" Christian, as set forth by the Lausanne Committee for World Evangelization (LCWE). She would no doubt be relegated to the latter category: one who gives "intellectual assent to basic Christian doctrines and claim[s] to be a Christian"—but is "a person who has not responded in repentance and faith to Jesus Christ as his personal Saviour and Lord."[2] The late John Stott called nominal Christianity "the great scandal of Christendom today."[3]

Most Christians of the Reformation era, however, did not testify to having "a transforming personal relationship with Christ,"[4] and Katie would have been among them. Religion was determined more by where a family lived than by personal profession of faith, an *oddity* introduced by Anabaptists. By virtue of marrying Martin Luther, Katie joined the Protestant ranks. That there is no evidence she actually made this new faith her own has gone essentially unnoticed by historians.

She was nevertheless the most indispensable figure of the German Reformation, save for Martin Luther himself. Take her and their twenty-year marriage out of the picture, and his leadership would have suffered severely. Had it not been for the stability she brought to his life, he may have gone off the rails emotionally and mentally by the mid-1520s. His emphasis on and modeling of marriage and family as an essential aspect of his reform would have been lost. Only Katharina von Bora—no other woman—could have accomplished what she did with this most unstable man. Without her, the Black Cloister would have gone to ruin—the result of which would have been no "table talk," and that is only the barest beginning of what would have been lost if she were taken out of the equation.

Although Martin's colleagues surely must have been at least unconsciously aware that she was the key to his emotional, mental, and financial stability, they were far more annoyed than appreciative of her commanding presence in his life. But the question remains, where would he have been without her? What if he had never married? What if he had married a sickly and submissive woman like Idelette Calvin? It is difficult to imagine him as the great Reformer he became.

And what about Katie? What if she had remained in the convent and had become a leading German abbess? What if she had left the convent but had remained single? What if women then were widely acknowledged as equals as they are today in Germany and in many other parts of the world? What if she had married a quantum chemistry professor who had not minded staying out of the spotlight while she pursued a political career? Might she have become a sixteenth-century version of Angela Merkel, Chancellor of Germany?

Such counterfactuals—the *what-ifs* of history—can shed light on an individual or heritage that can never be fully recovered. Still, when we hold out our flickering lanterns in the vast caverns of sixteenth-century Germany, we strain to accurately identify what meets our gaze.

So how does an author even begin to write a biography of Katharina von Bora? For me, it is a tenuous task of feeling my way into an already partially explored cave, looking for things others may not have seen. And I begin by recognizing the filter through which I see her.

In its literature, each century [since her birth] has portrayed Katharina von Bora through the filter of its own values. Luther's "Lord Katie" has been variously depicted as the First Lady of the Protestant parsonage, the Morning Star of Wittenberg, the businesswoman of the Reformation, a role model for working wives, the ideal wife and mother, a pig (in polemical satire), and a woman who exemplifies the inconsistencies of the transition between medieval and modern worldviews of women. Along with her husband, Katharina von Bora was satirized, vilified, idolized, revised, and fictionalized by contemporaries and later commentators. In all portrayals, her unique, strong personality, like Luther's, shines through.[5]

CHAPTER 1

"Jesus Cage"

INCARCERATION in a CLOISTER

Imagine a five-year-old girl going off to kindergarten, a half day of school. Not having attended preschool, she's frightened, crying, and hanging on to her mother for dear life. We've all witnessed such scenes. It's part of growing up. But what if the year is 1504, and the little girl is not headed for a three-hour morning session but rather to a lifetime of cloistered convent living? Today we would regard such treatment as serious child abuse. Not in the sixteenth century, however—unless a great Reformer rises up to make blistering attacks against this religious practice.

Sister Maria Deo Gratias, a consecrated nun with the Sisters of the Most Blessed Sacrament, was in sixth grade when she sensed her religious calling. When interviewed in 2014 for an article in the *New Yorker*, she spoke of the liberty in giving oneself "totally to God," insisting that the vow of chastity, almost universally regarded as limiting women's choices, actually opened the door to freedom. However, the four-year-old niece of one of the nuns was convinced these women lived in a "Jesus cage."[1] To a little girl, this is an understandable term—and a child's worst nightmare: to be kidnapped and incarcerated in a cage.

Katharina von Bora was five when she entered a "Jesus cage" in 1504 (a Benedictine cloister that also served as a boarding school for girls). Unlike Sister Maria, she had no opportunity to wait until she was

15

in sixth grade to sense a "religious vocation" and to later enjoy complete satisfaction inside the cloister, "stripped of everything that's not God."[2]

Katie, at five, was certainly not the youngest of girls to be dropped off at a convent. Edburga, a tenth-century English princess, entered a convent at age three. But the decision had been hers, so the story goes: "Her father set before her both religious objects (Bible, chalice, and paten) and secular (jewels, gold, and silver) . . . to decide the future course of her life." Without hesitation, the toddler chose the religious objects.[3] She remained in the convent her entire life, first a nun and then abbess of Nunnaminster. After her death, she was canonized a saint with a centuries-long cult following.

In Germany, too, there had been a long tradition of sending little girls to a convent. Indeed, the famed twelfth-century abbess Hildegard of Bingen was slotted for a religious vocation at age eight. Her situation was far more tenuous that that of Katie. A daughter of nobility, Hildegard was placed under the care of the anchoress Jutta, whose solitary cell was a small hut attached to the Benedictine monastery of Disibodenberg. Jutta practiced severe asceticism, including self-flagellation. Through her influence, Hildegard embraced the religious vocation.

Indeed, Katie's circumstances were not unusual during the Middle Ages. In her classic study, *Medieval English Nunneries*, Eileen Power tells of Guy Beauchamp, a fourteenth-century earl of Warwick, who took his two daughters, Margaret, age seven, and Katherine, age one, and left them at the Shouldham Priory to be trained for a religious vocation.[4] Katherine would become a nun, but no records remain of her older sister, who may have died young.

So, like many other young daughters of lesser nobility in this era, Katharina was carted off to a convent. In her case, the decision related to family circumstances. Her mother had died, and shortly thereafter her father made arrangements to marry a widow with children of her own. So her father packed her off to boarding school, perhaps with good intentions, but it effectively left her fatherless as well as motherless within a matter of months. In 1504, she arrived in Brehna to begin her education at the Benedictine cloister there. But one might wonder if she had actually been sold into monasticism, since the decision was primarily a financial one, as was true for many girls in late medieval times. Indeed, it was a common practice among cash-strapped lesser nobility in sixteenth-century Germany. For the recently widowed Hans von Bora, it meant one less child taking up space in a small house, one less mouth to feed, and one less dowry to be paid in the future. And it would also eliminate her from any inheritance. As in every case, there was a cost up front but that was negotiable. The amount paid for little Katie—a measly thirty groschen—could indicate either poverty or just plain stinginess.[5]

Born on January 29, 1499, near Leipzig, to Hans von Bora and Anna von Haugwitz, Katharina was a country girl with three brothers and perhaps a sister. Although the little *kindergartner*, as we imagine her, must have been filled with confusion and sadness during those first weeks and months away—no doubt missing her home and siblings—she may have quickly adjusted. Here the days were structured, and for a bright, quick-witted child with a love of learning, the school had much to offer—an excellent curriculum, spiritual nourishment, and proper grooming for a young lady.

How well Katharina acclimated emotionally as the months turned into years is not recorded. However, we do know Martin Luther's view of such customs. His assessment may have been based on Katharina's own recollections of her abandonment as a little child, which would one day lead to holy vows and life in a cloister. "It is very shameful that children, especially defenseless women and young girls," wrote Luther, "are pushed into the nunneries. Shame on the unmerciful parents who treat their own so cruelly."[6]

In 1524, the year after Katharina escaped the convent, Luther published a pamphlet, *A Story of How God Rescued an Honorable Nun, Accompanied by a Letter of Martin Luther to the Counts of Mansfield.* The tract consisted primarily of the testimony of Florentina, who was shipped off to a convent at age six. Five years later, she was forced to "take the veil." When she pleaded with her abbess to allow her to leave, she was ordered to do penance. Then when her efforts to contact her family and Luther himself were exposed, she was flogged and locked in a convent prison cell. It was only after she managed to flee that Luther published her first-person account, adding his own commentary. Her escape was the work of God, he insisted, and the cruel abbess was a Jezebel.[7]

Katharina was also groomed to "take the veil." Having barely reached her tenth birthday, the little girl bade good-bye to her schoolmates and friends and set out with strangers to live in a new home. She had no doubt been informed that her father had arranged for her to be relocated to Marienthron, a Cistercian cloister at Nimbschen. When she arrived, she must have realized immediately that her living situation had taken a major downward turn. The convent was smaller with fewer amenities. Housing, meals, and the inventory of books did not stack up to the well-endowed Benedictine compound at Brehna she had come to know so well. How much did she understand about this transfer? Did she realize that her father had decided she would live out her life as a cloistered nun?

There was a saying in early modern Germany: at ten a child (*kindische Art*), at twenty a maid, at thirty a wife, and so on. "To the people of the time, '*kindische Art*' expressed the incomplete development of body, mind, and moral faculties."[8] By the standards of her own day, not just ours, Katie was a child when she was taken to Nimbschen to begin the process of entering a lifelong vocation as a nun.

Perhaps she was too immature to fully comprehend what was going on. Perhaps she did understand and took the decision in stride, assuming her future vocation was a family tradition and it was her duty to carry it on. After all, two of her aunts, one from each side of the family, Magdalene von Bora and Margarete von Haubitz, were residents, the latter her abbess and superior. But did she really want to follow in their footsteps? Did she ever fantasize about the world outside?

About running away? Or did the deep moat and high fences around the perimeter of the compound give her pause?

Or perhaps she instinctively knew there was much to be commended in a religious vocation. Apart from the health perils, there were many drawbacks to marriage. It is no exaggeration to say that men were gross. Perhaps a prince took baths, wore clean clothes, and had mint to compensate for garlic breath. But the average man about town cared little for personal hygiene (at least in comparison to nuns), and on top of that, they treated women badly. A wife was fortunate not to be pushed around or beaten, and few wives escaped the coarse put-downs of a guffawing husband and his cohorts. Indeed, monastic life had its appeal.

There were many advantages for a girl who was placed in a convent. She was not forced into an arranged marriage with an old man or a younger man she found unappealing. She would not die prematurely in childbirth or be weighed down with household drudgery and the care of a house filled with hungry children. She would not be beaten by a violent husband because she did not do his bidding. She would have opportunities for education in a vocation that carried with it a certain prestige.

In the sixteenth century, there were no statistics of comparative life spans, but we now know that life for women in a convent was significantly healthier than life in the outside world. On average, an abbess lived well into her fifties, while the life span for most women outside the convent was under thirty. Nuns were expected to do manual labor and keep gardens, but there was considerable time devoted to the hours of prayer, meditation, reading, and choir—luxuries few women with families could afford. Cloistered nuns were less likely to die of contagious diseases so prevalent at the time, and for many nuns, a vegetarian diet was standard. However, it was not unusual for cloistered women, like women in the outside world, to complain about almost inedible food and the hunger pangs they suffered.[9] So we would be incorrect to imagine these nuns living in some sort of Renaissance spa.

The workday for nuns often carried a sense of accomplishment, whether laboring in their own garden plots, copying manuscripts, or producing psalters for daily convent use. In fact, "nuns in Germany," writes Judith Oliver, "made many psalters for their own use, despite repeated prohibitions against book production by women under Dominican supervision."[10] Most psalters were made by urban crafts-men, but nuns carried on this craft well into the sixteenth century, especially in Germany. The psalters were classified as "*nonnenbücher*" or "nuns' books." It was a pejorative term, and their craft was considered deficient in comparison to those made by professional bookbinders.[11] Today an original *nonnenbücher* would hardly be dismissed as inferior, either at a Sotheby's auction or at the Frankfurt Book Fair.

When Katharina escaped the convent, she was in some respects prepared for the outside world, having learned how to make do with very little and having mastered a wide range of skills that served her well as she stepped into the role of abbess of the Black Cloister. But her preparation went far beyond the basic functions of running a large household. There is every indication she was emotionally and mentally prepared as well. It is interesting that her escape involved what we might term a *sorority*. She was not one girl alone in the night, but rather part of a small, tight-knit group of *sisters* who told secrets and made clandestine plans.

But how were such plans accomplished? Like most cloisters of the time, silence was strictly observed—except, of course, for communal prayers and choir. But the nuns of Nimbschen, Ernst Kroker speculates, might have utilized a secret sign language to communicate, perhaps very well-honed gestures by the time it became necessary to plan their escape.[12]

Despite the rule of silence, it was not unusual for nuns to have best friends in the cloister and to become deeply attached emotionally, almost as though it were a romance—as it in fact sometimes was. Perhaps the most well-known such "romance" involved the celebrated abbess Hildegard of Bingen and a young nun, Richardis von Stade. Born in 1098, Hildegard's life would span most of the twelfth century.

She expressed her love for Richardis as an intimate friend and one who had encouraged her in her writing: "When I wrote the book Scivias, I bore a strong love to a noble nun . . . who suffered with me until I finished this book."[13]

In fact, their relationship was so passionate that other nuns became concerned. Hildegard poured out her heart to her beloved, alluding to this very unease among the other nuns: "I loved the nobility of your conduct, your wisdom and your chastity, your soul and the whole of your life, so much that many said: What are you doing?"[14]

Later when Hildegard learned that Richardis had been appointed abbess of another convent (a promotion arranged by her archbishop brother), she was heartbroken—and livid. She sought intervention from the pope, but to no avail. Some time later when word came that the young woman, only twenty-eight, was on her deathbed, Hildegard grieved in anger, blaming the untimely death on a prideful spirit and on the devil: "But the ancient serpent had attempted to deprive her of that blessed honor by assaulting her through her human nobility. Yet the mighty Judge drew this my daughter to Himself, cutting her off from all human glory."[15]

It is not difficult to imagine that Katharina missed the sisterhood and special friends who were left behind in the convent after her escape. Then as a busy *hausfrau*, there was no time for secret sisters, knitting groups, book clubs, and playful feminine banter.

Sisterhood, however, sometimes took a sinister turn, as when nuns fought among themselves or lashed out against an abbess or an outsider. Indeed, convents could be dangerous places for those who sought to clamp down on misbehavior or to institute new rules. When reform came to the diocese of Hildesheim in the mid-fifteenth century, father confessor Johann Busch was sent to the nuns of Derneburg. Among other changes, he insisted that all food must be held in common, including kegs of beer. To enforce this communal property directive, the priest asked to be taken to the cellar by one he thought to be a compliant sister. She courteously suggested he go first, as he later related:

Without thinking, I did so. But when I went down into it, she suddenly clapped to the door or vault over my head and stood upon it. I was shut up alone in there, thinking what would have happened if the nuns had shut me up there secretly . . . At length after some delay they opened the trap-door of the cellar and let me come out. After that I was never willing to go first into any closed place in any nunnery . . . The sister who did this was good enough and very simple, whence I was astonished that she should think of such a thing.[16]

In his effort to confiscate her beer, confessor Busch (no connection with Anheuser) may have imagined this clever nun to be simple. But we suspect otherwise.

As is true of all institutions, whether religious or secular, secret sins sometimes unravel and public scandals ensue. This has been true in the history of monasticism. Indeed, there were convents in medieval Europe that were thought to be little more than brothels. Luther himself had characterized convents with a slur that has resounded through the centuries: "worse than common brothels, taverns, or dens of thieves."[17]

Characteristic of Luther, he was grossly exaggerating, though if he had in mind the sixth-century Frankish convent at Poitiers, his assessment might have been fitting. The nun Chrodield and some forty followers staged a revolt against their abbess. Bishop Gregory of Tours offered his version of the uprising:

Chrodield, having collected about her . . . a band of murderers, wrong-doers, law-breakers, and vagrants of all kinds, dwelt in open revolt and ordered her followers to break into the nunnery at night and forcibly to bear off the abbess . . . The armed bands rushed in, ran about the monastery by the light of a torch in search of the abbess, and . . . carried off the prioress whom they mistook for the abbess in the darkness.[18]

Here we have a reverse rendition of the Keystone Kops. What a subject this would have been for a silent film! As Gregory reports, when Chrodield and her gang of nuns and thugs realized they had kidnapped the wrong woman, they returned and "secured the real abbess, dragged her away, and placed her in custody near the basilica of St. Hilary."[19]

Sixteenth-century accounts of rebel nuns were equally fascinating. In 1517, the very year that Luther was pounding nails into a church door, an English bishop sent an emissary to check out a small Benedictine convent near Somerset. The prioress, Katherine Wellys, had years earlier given birth to a daughter, the father of whom was a local chaplain who regularly spent the night with Katherine. But that was apparently the least of the problems. When it was time for the daughter to marry, Katherine dipped into the convent coffers for the dowry. Worse than that, the resident nuns' own allowances were being sent to the relatives of the prioress. So the nuns were living in a shabby dwelling, shivering without firewood and surviving on barely edible food and substandard ale. They were threatened that any form of whistle-blowing would be seriously punished. Indeed, they were terrified of Katherine.

When the bishop himself visited some months later, he learned that Elisabeth Wynter had been placed in stocks because of her "incorrigibility," only to escape with the assistance of three other nuns, having broken a window in the process. With nowhere to go, the nuns returned to the convent soon enough for Joanna Wynter, sister of the incorrigible nun, to go into labor and suffer the pains of childbirth. Hardly had the afterbirth been cleaned up when the prioress Katherine placed in stocks another nun who had not even been involved in the rebellion; and then she punched, beat, and kicked Elisabeth Wynter. All of this mayhem in contrast to the liturgy of the hours. At the end of the day, Juliana Bechamp, apparently only an observer of the mayhem, told the bishop, "I am ashamed to [be] here [under] the evil ruele [of] my ladye."[20]

Such shame would have been reason enough for Juliana to hitch a ride on a wagon load of herring barrels and make her escape. But what prompted Katharina von Bora to make that momentous decision? Was her decision based primarily on curiosity and excitement about the exhilarating new religious ideas emanating from Wittenberg? Was she intrigued by new notions of ecclesiology and biblical interpretation? And was there a sense that she was not finding fulfillment behind cloistered walls and simply wanted to be free? Imagine a Katharina von Bora not even able to speak and express her strong and articulate opinions. Were her words those of a twentieth-century Martin Luther generations hence? "Free at last! Free at last! Thank God Almighty, we are free at last!"[21]

The dysfunctional convents, of course, are the ones who easily grab our attention. But there is no reason to assume that most little girls like Katie who grew up to be nuns encountered such chaos or desired freedom in the outside world. Many of them were very satisfied with the silence behind cloistered walls. This was true of the nuns of St. Katharina in the town of St. Gall. In 1518, several years before Katharina herself would escape, Ulrich Zwingli began preaching and instituting reform in Switzerland. As a result, nuns were encouraged to abandon the convent. If they refused, they were required to leave the cloister and attend sermons delivered by Reformed preachers. The organist at the local cathedral described the situation:

> Then the women went forth shamefacedly two by two with the youngest in front according to age. But they showed little joy or eagerness: old, sick, limping women with great swollen eyes, for clearly they had found this going out a great hardship. It appears that those who were there would have preferred to stay separated from the world in their cloister until death. Otherwise they would have left [the house] before this, considering the quantity of scorn and denigration of their order that had been preached to them.[22]

The journal of Caritas Pirckheimer, who had entered the monastic system at age twelve, also reveals the predicament a loyal nun faced during the early years of the Reformation. Her entries span from 1524 to 1528 (the very years that Katharina was embarking on her new life). It was a perilous time for Caritas and her nuns, particularly as they were hearing reports from the outside world. Monks and nuns were being persecuted. Others simply "ran away from their cloisters and threw off their robes and habits."[23] Despite the pressure from Luther and his followers, Caritas and her nuns stood their ground:

> Many of the powerful as well as simple people came to their relatives who resided in our cloister. They preached to them and spoke of the new teachings and argued incessantly that the clois-tered were damned . . . [They] wanted to remove their children, sisters and aunts from the cloister by force and with many threats and also with many promises half of which, without doubt, they could hardly keep . . . The ferocious wolves, both males and females, came to my precious lambs, entered the church, drove out all the people and locked the church door, [arguing that] here their children were in the jaws of the devil, [the daughters responding] they did not want to leave the pious, holy convent. They were not in hell at all.[24]

Highly esteemed by Erasmus as one of the wisest women of the era, Abbess Caritas viewed the Reformation as evil and a serious threat to monastic life. There was nothing about the new teachings that tempted her. Schooled in Latin and the church fathers, she was in some respects a woman of the world, well-read and acquainted with literary figures and artists of the day, including Albrecht Dürer. Indeed, the German poet laureate Conrad Celtis labeled her the German Sappho. She was educated and articulate, and her journal offers a powerful record of events from the voice of a critic—and a woman. As abbess of the Convent of St. Clare's, she wrote of her clashes with the city council of Nürnberg, which supported Lutheran reform and sought to compel the convent to get in step with the times. Her refusal is recorded in sixty-nine short chapters that take the form of letters. She simply would not be cowed by upstarts seeking to split the church—the church she so dearly loved.

The oldest of twelve children, Pirckheimer (1467–1532) was in her fifties when Katharina and so many other nuns were leaving their monastic houses and habits behind. In her eyes, such nuns were denying the very foundations of faith and were forsaking the vows they had promised before God and Mother Church. Such activity was appalling—a nun divorcing Jesus, to whom she had pledged her troth.

For most nuns, rumors of religious revolution outside their bolted cloistered doors were nothing short of frightening. Life on the inside was routine. They were unprepared for the perils they learned of through personal testimonies. Mothers and sisters, aunts and cousins, had been widowed or died in childbirth or the plague, often leaving behind orphaned little ones. Life outside was grim.

Inside cloistered walls, nuns often enjoyed a certain amount of leisure—sometimes writing journals or devotionals, even theological or scientific treatises. And they read. Indeed, many were familiar with the newly discovered tenth-century popular German playwright Hrotsvitha of Gandersheim. One of her most often-cited scenes takes place in a convent and is as funny as it is serious. Here the predatory Governor Dulcitius sneaks into a convent in the dark of night to molest three *holy virgins* who run for cover into the kitchen. It might have ended badly for the nuns—as it often did—but not as we learn through the whispers of the holy virgins and the pen of Hrotsvitha: "Oh, look! He must be out of his senses! I believe he thinks that he is kissing us . . . Now he presses the saucepans tenderly to his breast, now the kettles and frying-pans! He is kissing them hard! . . . His face, his hands, his clothes! They are all as black as soot."[25]

Nuns may have feared such predatory outsiders, though not if they had a commanding abbess like Caritas Pirckheimer. If Katharina had perchance read this play (or saw it performed), we imagine she would have laughed heartily at this scene, as would have Martin Luther. Most of the writings of women religious, however, were devoid of humor.

Making fun of men, especially men in authority, was not typically an acceptable way for a nun to express herself. Although lacking in wit and humor, Pirckheimer left behind a fascinating journal about life in a sixteenth-century German convent. Katharina has left us nothing—at least nothing that was deemed worthy of saving.

In *Convent Chronicles*, Anne Winston-Allen asserts that rarely have voices of religious women been heard. Rather, we often learn about them in hagiographical accounts (legends of saints) typically penned by men. To truly understand them, we must go directly to their own writings and hear their own voices. Works relating to convents, for example, differ when the narrative is written by a man in authority from when written by a woman, whether an abbess or nun. In these writings, women are the subjects rather than objects. They show themselves as "self-determining, active agents, taking the initiative in solving the problems that face them. Collectively, they express a strong sense of self-worth and, in first-person narratives, indicate many forceful personalities."[26]

Problems that nuns encountered come to life very clearly in the narrative of Beel te Mushoel found in *Book of Sisters* (1503). Beel was sent to the Sisters of Common Life when she was fourteen. Her personality simply did not mesh with cloistered living: "For she had been high spirited and merry and now had to behave in a restrained, subdued manner. Oh, this life seemed so unsettling to her that her heart failed her when she thought that she must spend her life here."[27] She did, however, find that she was consoled by reading Scripture and by being the most industrious of the nuns in spinning and weaving. But still her personality was the wrong fit: "Thus her nature and this life were like light and darkness. And therefore she had a hard, difficult life and had to overcome her nature and break it."[28]

In Beel, we may have more than a glimmer of Katie von Bora's personality: high spirited and merry, industrious and finding it difficult to behave in a restrained, subdued manner. Katie escaped; Beel did not, though we are told that some time later, after consulting with a celebrated holy woman, Sister Beel's "heart became completely ignited by the love of God."[29] Such would not have been said of Katharina. "The darkness of history," writes Martin Treu, "weighs over the early years of Katharina von Bora."[30]

In some respects, Katharina's story parallels that of Patricia O'Donnell-Gibson, an ex-nun living today in southern Michigan. Though they are separated by centuries and circumstances of calling and convent life, I wonder if they might resonate with each other if language and time barriers were broken. Patricia grew up in a devout Irish Catholic family and felt the hand of God on her life when she was a young child. Then at seventeen, she experienced a profound sense of calling: "It followed me like the 'Hound of Heaven' all through the rest of my junior year." But she had questions: "Why me? . . . And the worst one—what would happen if I was supposed to go and didn't?"[31] After she graduated from high school, Patricia joined the Order of the Adrian (Michigan) Dominicans, where she slowly and arduously climbed the nunnery ladder.

Patricia tells her story in a book titled *The Red Skirt*. Her story is as dead serious as it is humorous. When she entered the convent, she left the world behind, including her short red skirt. "Hiding my butchered hair did nothing to heal the reality of my diminishing recognition of my female self," she writes. "Only my face and hands would be seen. I would not have children . . . I would keep my eyes down in modesty and purity, avoiding the gaze of men, and never bring attention to myself."[32]

Patricia escaped, not because she had turned her back on the Catholic Church; rather, the convent was too confining for her worldly ambitions, including having a family of her own. Today she is married, holds a master's degree, and has for three decades taught English literature. She and her husband live by a lake in Watervliet, Michigan. Together in their blended family they have two cats, seven children, and thirteen grandchildren.

It is not difficult to imagine Katharina as a young woman aware that her church was in desperate need of reform—that Johann Tetzel was little more than a sleazy con man making money off a mighty pyramid scheme, convincing gullible Christians to invest in indulgences for time off in purgatory. But had she also gotten wind of nuns and priests getting married in defiance of church order? Had she read Martin Luther's words on marriage, and his outcry against those who would forbid marriage? Luther insisted that the requirements of celibacy for priests and those in religious orders were instituted by Satan and regulated by rules that only benefited the church. He called on parents and friends of nuns to rescue them from their prisons, daring them to risk their very lives if need be.[33]

Did Katharina, like Patricia, find the convent too confining? Did she dream of having the freedom to walk about unencumbered to the downtown market and simply purchase a head of cabbage or to wear a red skirt? Did her maternal instincts cause her arms and breasts to ache with longings—longings to hold and nurse an infant? Did she want a more diverse life than could be had behind cloister walls? If only she had left behind a *Red Skirt* memoir. If only a musty, water-stained, handwritten package of papers buried in a crumbling old trunk had been picked up and left behind in a weatherworn German castle. If only new owners had pitched the detritus, leaving the pile at the end of their drive. If only a trash handler, moonlighting as a curious junk collector, spotted the bundle, there to find a strange manuscript: *Memoir of an Ex-Nun* by Katharina von Bora. If only . . .

"Here I Stand"

RELIGIOUS REVOLUTION IN GERMANY

It was a Wednesday, October 31, 1517," writes Tom Browning, "not really all that different from the thousands of other Wednesdays that had come before. It was fall, of course, and the air had cooled down and the leaves were putting on a wonderful show of color on the hillside along the River Elbe. It was a nice time to be a German. It was a nice time to live in rural Germany."[1]

The day was All Hallows' Eve, a day of commemoration of Catholic saints. We wonder what eighteen-year-old Katharina von Bora might have been doing that morning. Was she working in the convent garden, digging potatoes and turnips for winter storage in the cellar? Was she meditating on saints of long ago, unaware of what a motley crew they were—from desert hermits to violent crusaders and everything in between, including Saint Mary of Egypt, a one-time sex addict?

Wittenberg was a two-day journey away. There on that day, Martin Luther nailed ninety-five theses to the Castle Church door. Today this courageous act is the first thing many people think of in regard to the Protestant Reformation. However, that scholarly endeavor was not even the opening salvo, and it didn't generate a public response for several weeks. Only a historical perspective highlights the event. Contemporaries might have easily shrugged it off.

"There is properly no history," observed Ralph Waldo Emerson, "only biography." That has been my motto as a historian. I simply do not understand how historians can write and readers can enjoy history that does not have biography as its focus. The story of the Protestant Reformation in Germany is a case in point. It is one of the most captivating narratives in all of history. The cast of characters is made for a bestseller or an Academy Award–winning screenplay. And the lead characters—a monk with all the flair and flaws a writer could dream up and a cloistered nun escaping to freedom in the dark of night aboard a merchant's wagon—an audacious kidnapping and capital crime. There is romance (though not with each other) and marriage (though not the couples' first choice) and fumbling, lopsided sex (witnessed by curious onlookers) on the wedding night. And then what do they do but settle into housekeeping at the Black Cloister—the one-time home of black-robed monks. It just doesn't get any better than this.

But some of the stuff of this screenplay would need to be set aside. Even the least prudish among us today easily squirm when confronted with Martin Luther's crude remarks about the human body and his adolescent bathroom humor. It's the kind of trash talk found in movies that attract childish boys of all ages, who howl with laughter. Even most R-rated films leave such gratuitous juvenile humor on the cutting room floor.

Part of the appeal of the story is that Luther is an ordained minister—the very first *Lutheran* minister in history. He attacked his opponents with all the venom he could muster. His nickname for Pope Paul III was "His Hellishness," and when asked if the pope and those surrounding him were members of the body of Christ, he responded: "Yes, as much as spit, snot, pus, feces, urine, stench, scab, smallpox, ulcers, and syphilis are members of the human body."[2] Other sixteenth-century Reformers simply did not use such language. Nor did their anti-Semitism spill out in disgusting diatribes.

But like Luther, fellow Reformers certainly did inflame the passions of their followers to persecute fellow Christians. Luther's reform (along with that of Ulrich Zwingli in Zurich and John Calvin in Geneva) is viewed as part of the Magisterial Reformation that held high the concept of the state church. As such, many of the horrific Inquisition-type tactics of the Catholic Church would be left in place by the Reformers. Indeed, the "cruelest joke" of the Reformation was the drowning of Anabaptists (who affirmed believers' baptism and denied the efficacy of infant baptism). If they insist on rebaptism, so the joke went, we will do it for them. Many such believers in Zurich were executed in this manner, drowned in the River Limmat.

It would be left to Anabaptists to demand religious toleration and pave the way for the free-church movement that is characteristic of most evangelical churches today. In Strasbourg, however, Katherine Zell was holding forth for religious toleration, with scathing indictments against those responsible for burning at the stake the "poor Servetus" in John Calvin's Geneva. And she decried the persecution of Anabaptists, who were hunted as wild boars. But few other leaders among the Magisterial Reformers stood strong for religious toleration.

There are many things about Martin Luther we revere, but his manner and methods of reform were surely a mixed bag, making his bawdy jokes pale in comparison. His support of state-sponsored persecution, whether aimed at peasants or Jews or fellow Christians, was appalling, particularly in light of his understanding of Jesus and Paul. Referring to the execution of criminals (some who were "religious" criminals), Luther proclaimed, "The hand that wields the sword and strangles is . . . God's hand, and not the man but God hangs, breaks on the wheel, beheads, strangles, and makes war."[3] Harsh words. Yet this is the great father of the Protestant movement and in many respects the founder of "born again" evangelicalism. By 1519, he could affirm without reservation that righteousness is a "gift of God"—a gift received by faith: "Here I felt that I was altogether born again and had entered paradise itself through open gates."[4]

This is also the man to whom Katie would pledge her troth, for better and for worse. But before she showed up on the scene in Wittenberg, who was this man and what was this ongoing revolution that would transform her life? Unlike her, he was a commoner, his father a miner. The oldest of seven children born to Margarethe and Hans Luther, young Martin, like Katie, grew up quickly. At the age of five (the age when she would one day be dropped off at a convent), he was entering a nearby Latin school, and at fourteen (the age when she was preparing to take vows), he began studies at a boarding school operated by a monastic community known as the Brethren of the Common Life.

At eighteen, he enrolled at the University of Erfurt, where he excelled in his studies and dreamed of becoming a distinguished professor. But as the story goes, just two months after graduation, a thunderstorm stopped him dead in his tracks. When lightning struck nearby, he was certain the flash was a signal directed at him: *Become a monk or die.* So in this moment of terror, he promised Saint Anne (alleged mother of the Virgin and patron saint of miners) that he would become a monk. It was the kind of vow anyone at death's door might make—and break. But Martin turned his back on his scholarly aspirations, and in 1505, he entered the nearby Augustinian Black Cloister in Erfurt known for unusually strict discipline. His father was furious. His friends were shocked and confused, but they joined him for a farewell dinner on July 17, 1505. After walking to the monastery door, he parted from them with somber words: "This day you see me, and then, not ever again."[5]

One year earlier, five-year-old little Katie—with no friends, no farewell dinner—had also entered a cloister. Martin entered by choice with his eyes wide open. Katie was confused and abandoned, like any kindergartner would be in such circumstances. In 1507, Martin was ordained a priest. For Katie, the next big event would be her transfer from the Benedictine cloister in Brehna to Marienthron, a Cistercian monastery in Nimbschen. They were on parallel tracks in ministry, separated by some sixteen years in age and by more than one hundred miles' distance. Both possessed a budding sense of confidence. The future held opportunities for them to make their mark. He would one day become a noted monastic leader; she perhaps like her aunt would end her years as an abbess. For both of them, the decade that followed involved loyal ministry in the Catholic Church.

Then at the very moment Martin Luther began his revolution in Wittenberg in the autumn of 1515, Katie von Bora, having completed her year of probation, was reciting her marriage vows to Jesus, promising to be true, until death do them part. Let this be one more amusing—albeit less than resolutely factual—helping of lore dished up by historians. Indeed, historians have challenged the veracity of the story of young Luther promising Saint Anne he would become a monk at the very moment he was struck down by lightning. So also that he actually grabbed the closest hammer and nailed a long parchment list of ninety-five theses to the Castle Church door. And who knows, there may have been a cosmic moment in time on a certain lovely autumn day in 1515 when commitments to and from the church intersected. Like other examples of Luther lore, this tale does contain more than a kernel of truth.

On October 8, 1515, Katharina was "married" to Christ, consecrated as a nun. At the same time, some fifty-two miles away in Wittenberg, Martin was presenting far-reaching insights on the book of Romans. These lectures launched a biblical upheaval that would roll through the centuries, swaying the hearts and minds of students and disciples. He not only transformed humdrum, centuries-old writings into stunning good news, but he would also set a precedent for studying, exegeting, interpreting, and translating the Bible. And not just translating, but encouraging laypeople to read it. Who could have imagined the sweeping consequences? From the pope and the emperor on down, the Bible became a book to be reckoned with—a book, not simply the teaching of one man whose *conscience was captive to the Word of God.*

Luther insisted he did not wish to establish a new church or start a Reformation: "I simply taught, preached, and wrote God's Word; otherwise I did nothing. And then, while I slept, or drank Wittenberg beer with my Philip [Melanchthon] and my [Nicolaus von] Amsdorf, the Word so greatly weakened the papacy that never a prince or emperor did such damage to it. I did nothing. The Word did it all."[6]

The good news that Martin Luther found in Romans in 1515 would, from this time forward, be preached in churches and cathedrals and studied in small groups. One such occasion was a spring evening in 1738, 223 years later, when John Wesley's heart was strangely warmed. "I went very unwillingly to a society in Aldersgate Street, where one was reading Luther's preface to the Epistle to the Romans. About a quarter before nine," Wesley confessed, "while he was describing the change God works in the heart through faith in Christ, I felt my heart strangely warmed. I felt I did trust in Christ alone, for salvation; and an assurance was given me that He had taken away my sins, even mine, and saved me from the law of sin and death."[7]

Luther's biblical teachings and translation would reverberate far beyond the borders of what we know as Lutheranism, turning him into a giant figure in the history of world religions. Others before him had taught justification by faith, but no one forged and fired and hammered passages in Romans into fine gold as he did. The just shall live by faith—faith alone, not by works, not by the filthy rags of righteousness. In Sunday school, we memorized one verse after another from Romans, and Luther was our hero. Paul too. But Luther was more Pauline than Paul himself. *The just shall live by faith*, a single sentence that stands above all others in all sixty-six books of the Bible. Indeed, Luther was the one who brought those thundering words into my world of the little Green Grove Alliance Church in northern Wisconsin. Luther was the one who taught us that, unlike those Catholics who rode the school bus with us, we wouldn't be going to hell for believing in salvation by works.

But do the just truly live by faith *alone—sola fide*? Although a hallmark of the Reformation, many argue (both Protestants and Catholics) that it is not an entirely biblical doctrine. The actual text in Romans 1:17 reads, "The righteous will live by faith," and Luther alone added the word *alone*. It stuck. Faith *alone*. He was certainly not above exaggeration, and perhaps that also included his exegesis.

His discovery of justification by faith had above all else challenged his own spiritual path—that of striving to earn salvation through good works. He was terrified of going to hell because of unconfessed sins. Indeed, he thoroughly exasperated his confessor, Johann von Staupiz, who reportedly scolded: "Look here, brother Martin: If you're going to confess so much, why don't you go do something worth confessing? Kill your mother or father! Commit adultery! Quit coming in here with such flummery and fake sins!"[8] But even while Luther was praying, fasting, and confessing for hours on end, he was at times raging against God: "I did not love, indeed I hated, that God who punished sinners."[9]

Luther was as complicated as was the revolution he spawned. By 1515, while teaching and preaching the gospel he discovered in Romans, he was still a monk on the make, having been appointed supervisor of a dozen monasteries. He seems to have worked nonstop. In a letter to John Lange, prior of Erfurt, he vented his frustration:

> I have need of two secretaries, and do almost nothing all
> day long but write letters . . . I am convent preacher; reader at
> meals; I am required to preach every day in the parish church;
> I am director of studies . . . I am vicar of the Order, i.e. prior
> eleven times over; I have to superintend the Leitzkau fish pond;
> I have charge of our people of Herzberg at Torgau; I lecture on
> St. Paul, and collate the Psalms.[10]

Although a busy man, he was not too busy to identify, write down, and publish ninety-five theses in the autumn of 1517. And with that accomplished, the Reformation bell would begin to peal—a bell that would continue to ring out for centuries to follow. A well-known quote from Karl Barth could more aptly apply to Martin Luther: "As I look back upon my course, I seem to myself as one who, ascending the dark staircase of a church tower and trying to steady himself, reached for the banister, but got hold of the bell rope instead."[11]

Calls for revival, renewal, and reformation have over the centuries popped up like crocus blooms in springtime. Even today, there are those who claim to be carrying out a new Reformation. But never has Christianity seen a religious reformation of historic proportions like the one that rocked the sixteenth century. There were dozens of great religious leaders who were contemporaries of Martin Luther, as well as hundreds before and after. But he alone fit the bill as *the* great Reformer. Sure, the times were right. Sure, someone else would have come along. But no one else had the intellect and personality to carry it out, with its three most critical components: biblical teachings and translation; daring disputations on wide-ranging church traditions; and, most scandalous of all, clerical marriage demonstrated by his own public marriage to Katharina von Bora.

Until October 31, 1517, Martin Luther was not known beyond Wittenberg. In 1511, he had traveled to Rome on official monastic business, but left as anonymously as when he had arrived. Disillusioned with the shameless impiety of the holy city, he would later see that the trip had a formative influence on his thinking. Back in Germany, he quickly became recognized as a brilliant monk. In 1512, he was invited to become a professor at the University of Wittenberg, specifically in the field of biblical studies. He was in his element, teaching and learning at the same time. "Luther set himself to learn and expound the Scriptures," writes Roland Bainton. "On August 1, 1513, he commenced his lectures on the book of Psalms. In the fall of 1515 he was lecturing on St. Paul's Epistle to the Romans. The Epistle to the Galatians was treated throughout 1516–17. These studies proved to be for Luther the Damascus road."[12]

He might have remained a monk professor the rest of his life. Indeed, it is difficult to imagine how his future would have unfolded had not the Catholic Church found itself deeply in debt in rebuilding the most celebrated landmark of Renaissance architecture—St. Peter's

Basilica in Rome. A battle was looming, though hardly between Martin and Michelangelo. The eventful year was 1516. Enter Johann Tetzel, sent by Rome to sell indulgences for cold, hard cash. Tetzel had personality and a cool jingle: "As soon as the coin in the coffer rings, the soul from purgatory springs." Actually the jingle may be pure legend, but it has served historians for centuries.

Luther's ninety-five theses, written in Latin, were meant to be a disputation to be discussed primarily by scholars who had shown interest in reforming the church. We often imagine that the bell rang on Halloween night, and by the next morning most of Germany was ready to take down the papacy. Not so. It wasn't until more than two months later that friends translated his theses into German and printed them as a pamphlet for wide distribution. Then the wheels began to turn. The pamphlets quickly made their way around Germany and beyond the borders. The ringing bell could never be unrung.

Now eighteen, what did nun Katie know about these ninety-five theses? It is not difficult to imagine that merchants making deliveries might have been curious to see how a cloistered woman on kitchen duty would react to this storm raging right outside her convent walls. Did she read a printed pamphlet during the winter months of 1518? If so, we can only imagine her heart pounding—fear combined with cautious excitement.

All the while, as Luther continued to teach and publish his lectures, the pope essentially ignored the little dustup in Germany. He did, however, direct theologians to challenge and to question the monk. But Luther was quick to respond. When he was questioned by Cardinal Cajetan in Augsburg in the summer of 1518, he did more than wonder aloud if the pope might be the antichrist. He likewise refused to recant his writings against the church. For such, he should be burned at the stake. But before that cagey cat Cajetan rounded up his henchmen and pronounced the verdict in the morning, the mouse Martin had slipped away in the night. In the summer of 1519, Luther took the stage to debate the brilliant professor Johann Eck, who came face-to-face with

Luther in Leipzig. Hot topics were on the docket, including purgatory, papal authority, penance, and the sale of indulgences—all key elements of Catholic tradition. Without biblical support, Luther argued, they were indefensible. Again a cagey cat set a trap, but before the mouse could be caught, he slipped out of sight.

By now, the news was seeping through the gates and barred windows of even the most tightly cloistered convents. What was Katie thinking? Had she heard about the audacious monk who dared to debate the noted professor from Ingolstadt University and that the streets of Leipzig were packed? Incredible events were passing her by. Nothing like this had happened before. Who was this monk who had been accompanied by two hundred armed students? Social media whispers must have been shocking—and dreadfully slow in coming. Once again, the monk not only pounded nail holes through indulgences and purgatory, but also through papal infallibility and the power of the church. Before the two-week drama had ended, before the curtain calls were over and the crowds could cheer him on, he was gone.

But in this debate, more than in any other forum, he had been exposed. His heresy hung in the air—stark naked sacrilege without even a papal pallium to cover his blasphemy. The pope took notice and took his time. Not until the summer of 1520 did Leo X issue his now-infamous bull, *Exsurge Domine*, threatening the monk with excommunication. In vintage Luther style, the monk gathered friends and supporters and burned it. The bull had called on faithful Catholics to rise up in opposition to this wild boar. There is no hard evidence, but perhaps the papal bull was read aloud before morning prayers at the convent of Marienthron? Which camp would Katie have joined—the side of the bull or the side of the boar? The opening words of the papal bull read as follows: "Arise, O Lord, and judge thy cause. A wild boar has invaded thy vineyard. Arise, O Peter, and consider the case of the Holy Roman Church, the mother of all churches, consecrated by thy blood."[13] The papal bull further stipulated that Luther's books were to be burned.

On a cold January day in 1521, Martin Luther was excommunicated. Then came the emperor's summons to appear before the Diet of Worms. Here Luther was expected to recant what he had written, by this time an impressive body of work. But once again the Catholic cat (in the form of Emperor Charles V) will fail to catch the mouse. "All Germany is up in arms against Rome," wrote the papal envoy Jerome Alexander. "I cannot go out in the streets but the Germans put their hands to their swords and gnash their teeth at me." The Imperial legates, however, seemed to be playing a game of psychological warfare. Most of three months were consumed with mundane business before Luther was called upon to recant—three months of misery to mull over a slow and excruciating death by fire. When ordered to recant, he was sorely tempted, and at first he faltered. On the second day, however, his courage returned. No, he would not recant. He made his case, ending with those ever-memorable lines. Fact or fiction, they live on as the chorus of the fight song that split the Catholic Church:

> My conscience is captive to the Word of God.
> I cannot and I will not recant anything,
> for to go against conscience is neither right nor safe.
> [Here I stand, I cannot do otherwise.]
> God help me. Amen.[14]

With no other choice, the emperor issued the Edict of Worms, condemning Martin Luther as a heretic. He was now an outlaw. The penalty, death by burning. But once again, with the help of friends, including Prince Frederick the Wise, he slipped out of town—kidnapped during the night and taken to the secluded Wartburg Castle. Does the full report filter into cloistered convents, or does Katharina hear only half the story? Does she imagine the audacious monk is dead?

For his own safety, Luther remained incarcerated at the Wartburg for nearly a year. His emotional state might almost suggest bipolar disorder—highs of almost unstoppable productivity and a sense of accomplishment, and lows of depression and apathy. On the positive side, he translated the New Testament into vernacular German and wrote essays, and thus that time was critical for his own development and for the progress of the Reformation.

During these early years of the Reformation, Philip Melanchthon and several others worked alongside Luther in Wittenberg, sometimes giving advice that he contemptuously ignored. There were others who supported him at a distance, including Argula von Grumbach (von Stauffer). She also stood before princes in defense of his teachings, appearing before the Diet of Nuremberg in 1523. Though often ignored by historians, her willingness to risk everything for the Reformation illustrates how profoundly the gospel message had captured the hearts and minds of vastly diverse individuals.

Born and marrying into German nobility, Argula's worldview, social status, and a history of family intrigue were very different from those of either Martin or Katie. We shake our heads and wonder why this wife and young mother of four would lay everything on the line to take a public stand. She was aware that her husband's court appointment was in jeopardy because of her speaking out in support of Luther, but her sense of duty trumped her family's financial welfare and social status. If God cares for the birds and the flowers of the field, he would care for her family. Her defense of Luther and Melanchthon, she insisted, was no more than defending the Word of God itself.

The issue that most roused her ire and brought her before the Diet of Nuremberg was the arrest and exile of a student supporter of Luther. She argued from Scripture that he was clearly no heretic, but her words were dismissed as those of a woman, worse, an "insolent daughter of Eve." The princes who might have at least listened to her arguments, she wrote, regarded "the Word of God no more seriously than a cow does a game of chess."[15] Her support of Luther's teachings, however, was taken very seriously, and Luther recognized that. In a letter to a friend, he wrote:

The Duke of Bavaria rages above measure, killing, crushing and persecuting the gospel with all his might. That most noble woman, Argula von Stauffer, is there making a valiant fight with great spirit, boldness of speech and knowledge of Christ . . . Her husband, who treats her tyrannically, has been deposed from his prefecture . . . She alone, among these monsters, carries on with firm faith, though, she admits, not without inner trembling. She is a singular instrument of Christ.[16]

During the six years she remained cloistered after 1517, was Katie longing to be in on the action? Was she craving for news and hearsay that seeped into the convent? Nothing like this had happened during her lifetime, and heretics like the fifteenth-century Jan Hus were hardly the stuff of saintly hagiography. Did she know that all Germany was up in arms—that her own people were gnashing their teeth at Catholic envoys? What would happen to her? We may be on the mark if we suspect that this determined woman, later known as Frau Luther, was chomping at the bit to be out in the streets herself. When she did break free, she would not be confronting cows at a Nuremberg diet as did Argula, but she would never be out of earshot of the latest news.

The aspect of the Luther revolution that no doubt most piqued Katie's interest was that which related to clerical celibacy and marriage. Truly, this aspect of the sixteenth-century Reformation was as stunning as was his scriptural stance against indulgences and papal authority. Married clerics? The idea was preposterous. But marriage and procreation were part and parcel of Luther's gospel message. Monks and nuns were now duty bound to kiss the convent good-bye. His language, as we have seen, was shocking. He declared that monasteries and convents were the very opposite of what they claimed to be. They were "worse than common brothels, taverns, or dens of thieves"—not institutions enhancing spirituality and devout living. Families, he insisted, have the responsibility to free their daughters.[17]

Imagine how such words might astound a nun who as a virgin had pledged to be married to Christ and to remain so the rest of her life. Scandalous, to be sure. To accept the gospel as Luther had set forth was radical enough, but to abandon her vows and convent—how could she?

Luther's utter scorn of clerical celibacy might be best summed up in the personal admissions of one of his bitterest rivals. Not Pope Leo X or one of his representatives, but another Magisterial Reformer, Ulrich Zwingli, across the Swiss border in Zurich. When Zwingli was about to move up the priestly career ladder and take over the pulpit of the local cathedral, people began to whisper about his seduction of the daughter of a local official. On examination, he admitted his shortcomings, but emphasized that he clearly had standards: "My principle was to inflict no injury on any marriage . . . and not to dishonour any virgin nor any nun." In fact, he could prove it: "I can call to witness all those [women] among whom I have lived."[18]

In some settings, such an admission would have been sufficient to stop the process. But as it turned out, the only other candidate the church was considering had fathered six children. Zwingli got the job. His ministry there would continue for more than a dozen years, until his death in 1531. Along the way, he preached against enforced clerical celibacy—a stance considered then to be a radical notion. And again he was engulfed in scandal. That a priest would have a live-in housekeeper to cook and wash clothes seemed fair enough. Anna Reinhard was a widowed mother of three. When she became pregnant with her fourth child in 1522, he did what was right and married her, albeit secretly. When his enemies found out, they cried foul. Everyone knew that "celibate" clerics fathered children left and right. Clerical marriage, however, was the serious scandal.

So in many respects, Martin Luther's stance against clerical celibacy was the most radical aspect of his reform. His scriptural writings were a natural outgrowth of his teaching, and his translation of the New Testament into German was a reasonable next step. His raging against indulgences was an obvious reaction to Tetzel's selling of salvation. But clerical marriage? How could the church carry on if the pope and cardinals and clergy on down had wives and children to inherit its vast stores of wealth? The problems were already nearly out of hand with the succession of the Renaissance Borgia popes. What would happen if parish priests and monks began passing church property on to their children?

Clerical marriage was, according to Reformers, a matter of morality. Katherine Schütz Zell (two years older than Katie) expressed this loud and clear when she married a priest from Strasbourg, Matthew Zell. But her rationale that marriage "uplifted the moral degradation of the clergy" fell on deaf ears. Luther, however, was louder than she was. *Shut down the convents. Empty out these brothels,* he thundered. (In medieval times, brothels were sanctioned by the church—even now in the 1520s.) But Luther's cry for reform was not aimed at prostitutes. It came straight from Genesis—to become one flesh in marriage and to be fruitful and multiply. It was aimed particularly at nuns residing in cloistered convents, with little hope of breaking free. Imagine nuns hearing such language. It would have been difficult to remain neutral.

Would Katie stand her ground and resist any attempt to shut down the only way of life she had ever known? Or would she, like other anonymous German nuns, cut all ties to convent life? Would she tiptoe down the hallway and slip out the door in the predawn hours and climb aboard a herring wagon? It was an exhilarating and dangerous time to be alive. Staying or leaving was a decision that, either way, carried critical consequences.

Luther was the man of the hour. No other Reformer was prepared to raise the stakes so high and call for monks and nuns to flee their monasteries and marry. Reform to be sure—reform that would stand the test of time, with a very distinct revolutionary cast. Kimberly Kennedy writes:

> In 1530, the Augsburg Confession, the foundational Lutheran statement of faith, affirmed and made official Luther's rejection of monastic vows . . . Thus monasticism, despite its auspicious

beginnings, great heroes, and impressive accomplishments, served primarily to obscure the truly important truths of the Christian faith. It ensnared the ignorant . . . as well as sincere converts, in a corrupt discipline not unlike "a carefully planned prison," while preaching that its rigorous "show" was the superior form of a Christian life and service.[19]

While he preached God's blessings on priests, monks, and nuns who married, Martin Luther himself vowed to remain single. No one would lure him into the marriage bed. No one—until an escaped nun still in love with another man made a proposal too good to refuse.

CHAPTER 3

"A Wagon Load of Vestal Virgins"

ESCAPING THE CONVENT

No modern nun would be caught dead fleeing a convent in the middle of the night, hidden among herring barrels and transported in a wagon pulled by a team of horses over a bumpy dirt road. Escaping in a convertible, hair flying (cropped though it may be), is the only way to go. So it was for Patricia O'Donnell-Gibson (who, as we learned in chapter 1, lives today with her husband in southern Michigan). For Katie von Bora, however, a horse-drawn wagon was the only convertible available. Unlike Katie, Patricia entered the convent at seventeen on her own accord. Stories of devout missionary nuns had sparked her own sense of calling. But she soon began to realize that the cloistered life did not suit her. After six years, and with the knowledge of her mother superior, Patricia left her life as a nun behind.[1] For Katie, the risks were higher, and the culture shock far greater.

Sending a girl off to a convent at a young age with the assumption that she would take her vows in her mid-teens does not automatically lead to spiritual maturity. Indeed, there is widespread evidence that many nuns throughout the Middle Ages had discovered that monasticism was not necessarily the way to find union with God. Martin Luther cynically suggested that "if ever a monk got to heaven by his monkery it was I."[2] Implying that no one had exceeded him in performing the dutiful works of a monk—works that in the end would count for nothing.

Katharina left no comparable negative reflections of her years as a nun. In fact, she would later imply that she was closer to God as a nun than living in the world. Indeed, the only hint of dissatisfaction is that she simply agreed to the escape plan. There is no indication she was the instigator of the plot or even was in on the planning committee. Unlike Luther, who led the charge as a religious revolutionary, she may have joined the jail breakers for freedom, and no more. We do know she respected Magdalene von Staupitz, the oldest of the runaway nuns. As early as 1516, "Magdalene had received some of Luther's writings and had eagerly imbibed the Reformed doctrines,"[3] writes J. H. Alexander. She appears to have been the instigator of the plot, and somehow she secretly convinced eleven younger nuns to join her. She must have known them well. Even just one of them who had second thoughts could have derailed the entire scheme.

Years ago, I interviewed Kenneth Lanning, who was then heading an FBI task force investigating claims of satanic ritual murder. Many of the accounts featured fantastic conspiracies involving dozens of people. It's possible to keep secret a crime involving one person, he told me, but as soon as two or three or a dozen are in on the conspiracy, the odds of secrecy are progressively and drastically reduced. In the case of the escaped nuns, we have a dozen in on the plot. This story is truly amazing. Twelve nuns having pledged themselves as virgins, Jesus their spouse, all remain tight-lipped—not one backing out or getting cold feet.

We so easily imagine that the nuns planned their getaway and snuck out in the night, summing it up as an exciting and amusing caper. We forget how truly astonishing were the conspiracy and the successful escape. This was, in fact, one of the most stunning jailbreaks in history. How, we wonder, were they able to so perfectly plan and execute this clandestine plot? In most of the accounts of this daring feat, men from the outside are given credit, while the cleverly executed scheme of the nuns is passed over. One online site sums up this "extraordinary stunt" as a passive activity of "having the ladies smuggled out."[4] Hardly.

Another mystery is why not one of those nuns later recorded what had gone on in the secret planning sessions and on the night of the escape. Or maybe someone did. What if there actually exists a scrap of paper containing two journal entries penned by Katharina, one undated, the other dated April 5, 1523? It would be a most valuable discovery. We would certainly pore over every word. And here we have it. First, a one-sentence lament before she escaped: "My spirit grieves at the thought of ending my days in this dreary place—dead, while yet I am living."[5] And the second, a detailed reflection on the getaway:

> It was Easter Eve in the year 1523 . . .
>
> Slowly the twilight fell upon the earth . . .
>
> The night was damp and cold. A bitter wind drove the ragged clouds across the face of the moon, whose pale beams threw ghostly shadows upon the earth. In the forest the trees groaned and creaked, their branches tossed by the gale.
>
> A great wagon, loaded with barrels, moved slowly along the road . . .
>
> Again the screech-owl shrieked. No other sound was heard, save the creaking of the branches in the wind. In wild haste [we] slipped down, and crept along the wall . . .
>
> After a few hours, when the sky grew rosy in the east, and the first fiery ray of the Easter sun broke upon the earth, new life stirred [us] with irresistible force, and as with one voice, the exultant strain burst forth from [our] lips:
>
> > "Christ the Lord is risen
> > From His martyr prison,
> > Let us all rejoice in this,
> > Christ our joy and solace is,
> > Kyrie eleison."[6]

Alas, these are the translated words of Armin Stein, taken from his contrived Victorian-era novel, hardly Katie's plainspoken German. Disregard the creaking branches, the screech owls, squeaking wagon wheels, and ghostly shadows. Indeed, by the time the bone-weary nuns arrived in Torgau, they were frightened and dirty, and all they must have wanted was a bath and a bed. And sadly, no scrap of paper has been discovered that even hints at their hardship. If ever written down, we must remember that women's written words counted for little and often found their place amid the trash.

The nuns had no doubt learned as much about Martin Luther and the Reformation through the grapevine as did the average person on the street. On her own initiative, Magdalene apparently had contacted Luther requesting his help in executing their plan for escape. He had called for this very kind of subversive activity, probably never imagining he would actually be expected to become involved in this conspiracy to commit a capital crime. Although Luther had insisted family members should be the ones to free their daughters, arguing that it was "a godly action and perfectly safe," it was, in fact, a very dangerous activity; a year after these nuns had escaped, a man elsewhere in Germany was executed for this very crime.[7]

Now Luther, having barely escaped the death penalty himself (hiding out at the Wartburg Castle for nearly a year), was risking his life again. Having returned to the Black Cloister and facing an impossibly hectic schedule, he now felt obligated to set in motion a plan for someone from the outside to assist the runaway nuns. Did he ever shake his head and say with a sigh, *Good God, what have I gotten into?* Did he even know exactly where the convent was located? Was he told it was on an isolated tract of land, a distance of more than seventy miles of rough roads through heavily forested terrain? But it was a small world. He was well acquainted with the brother of the nun who initiated the escape, and he just happened to know of a trusted vendor who made deliveries to that very spot.

Leonard Koppe was a merchant and city councilman who resided in Torgau, located roughly between the convent and Wittenberg. He agreed, with the help of a nephew and a friend, to take the risk of kidnapping the nuns, though not without a certain amount of persuasion from Luther. Luther insisted that nuns should, if they wished, simply be permitted to depart from the convent in an honest and orderly way. It was therefore a Christian act of mercy to kidnap a nun, which became a key part of his reform. Catholics, however, considered the breaking of a vow a mortal sin, and kidnapping a capital crime.

Although a far lesser story of conspiracy, the kidnapping of Clare of Assisi is an interesting comparison. Clare was born some three hundred years before Katie. She was a seventeen-year-old daughter of nobility who surreptitiously made plans to be kidnapped by Francis, who was more than a dozen years her senior. Though she did not hide in a wagonload of herring barrels and did not escape on Easter, she did make a run for it on Palm Sunday. Headed in opposite directions, both young women connived in underhanded schemes—Katie abandoning the cloistered life, Clare embracing it. In the centuries since, the names Francis and Clare have been bound together, as though *Saint* were their first names. So also Martin Luther and Katharina von Bora, though minus any association with sainthood. Despite his involvement in kidnapping a young woman, it is interesting that Francis, second only to the Virgin Mary, is probably the most popular saint—and garden statue—today.

Had the twelve nuns who escaped the Marienthron convent each been asked to give a reason for fleeing, would they have agreed with Luther that it was impossible to be chaste in the convent? Or would they simply have admitted that they wanted out of the dull and dreary life they were living—that the grass was greener on the other side of the high fence, that they wanted to be part of the action, and that they desired a family of their own? Bumping along on the rutted roads, however, the future may have seemed very uncertain—feelings of excitement tangled up with fear and second thoughts.

For Protestants today, if they ever contemplate this episode of the

Reformation, it is a grand salvation story. If we were to view Martin Luther as the Christ figure, the nuns represent the twelve disciples: Magdalene von Staupitz (the Peter figure), Else, Lanita, Ave, Margarete, Fronika, Margarete, Katharina, Ave, and three others so obscure they remain nameless. Like these nuns, the twelve in the Gospels were less than faithful and were often gripped by fear and uncertainty.

Hidden beneath the covered herring wagon, the nuns could not have imagined themselves as twelve disciples. They were perhaps as embarrassed as they were relieved to find a safe haven, first in Torgau and the next day in Wittenberg. How does an exhausted nun in full habit (or a nightgown) alight gracefully from a wagon with sideboards? What a spectacle it was—a spectacle captured in Wittenberg by a student writing to a friend: "A wagon load of vestal virgins has just come to town, all more eager for marriage than for life. God grant them husbands lest worse befall."[8] The term "vestal virgins" may have been used to add a touch of humor, but these nuns were nothing like the ancient Roman beauties—virgins who tended the eternal fire of Vesta, goddess of hearth and home. Katie, like most of the women in the wagon, would soon enough lose her virginity and become a very down-to-earth *goddess* of hearth and home.

Hardly had the news gotten out when the backlash began. Catholic leaders and laypeople alike deplored the kidnapping of nuns. Indeed, the backlash continues today. The website Catholic Apologetics Information contains an article by Michael Baker, titled "[What] Was Luther Really Like, After All?" in which he cites a common quotation by Jacques Maritain, a twentieth-century French Catholic philosopher:

> After a rape of nuns which took place on the night of Holy Saturday, 1523, Luther calls the citizen Koppe who organised the exploit, a "blessed robber," and writes to him, "Like Christ, you have drawn these poor souls from the prison of human tyranny. You have done it at a time providentially indicated at that moment of Easter when Christ destroyed the prison of His own." He

himself was surrounded by nuns thus restored to nature. His [wife] Catherine Bora was one of them. It is curious to note that a base contempt for womanhood is the normal price of this war against Christian virginity.[9]

In a letter to George Spalatin several days later, Luther described the nuns as a "wretched group." Pleading for financial aid, he continued: "I feel very sorry for them . . . This sex, which is so very weak by itself and which is joined by nature, or rather by God, to the other sex, perishes when so cruelly separated."[10] (He did not yet know the strength of Katharina.) After they had arrived safely, Luther thanked Koppe, commenting that his part in the rescue of the nuns would long be remembered.

We read about the predawn escape, but little appears to be known about those left behind. Soon afterward, however, the abbess and abbot contacted Elector Frederick, complaining that his subjects had been responsible for ruining the convent. He responded on June 13: "Since we do not know how this happened and who incited the girls from the convent to undertake this, and since we have never dealt with this and similar matters before, we leave it to their own responsibility."[11]

It was considered a tragedy that the convent in Nimbschen had "lost half of its residents within two years" (twelve on Easter 1523, and three more on Pentecost; still others followed soon after). The situation wreaked havoc on this small convent and elsewhere: "At the end of 1525 there were only twenty nuns in Nimbschen . . . Throughout the country, the 'exodus' had begun."[12] And with the exodus came exaggerated stories of monastic abuse.

In fact, over the centuries, accounts of nuns liberated from convent prisons were matched only by claims of kidnapped nuns who were loath to leave. Through generations, the stories multiplied and in the process created serious religious tension—and not just in Europe. In 1834, the story of Sister Mary John, who had purportedly attempted to escape, fueled the burning down of a convent outside Boston. Two years later, a bestselling book appeared that claimed to be a true story of a nun in Montreal: *Awful Disclosures of Maria Monk, or, The Hidden Secrets of a Nun's Life in a Convent Exposed.* Convents were worse than common brothels, Luther had declared. The fictionalized Maria is depicted in full habit holding her baby. Not that nuns never had babies. But these lurid stories sparked fires of rage.

The all-too-real account of Margaret de Prestewych dates to the late fourteenth century. The setting was Lichfield, England, more than a century before Katharina was born. "It is satisfactory to know," writes Eileen Power, "that one energetic girl at least succeeded in making good her protests and in escaping from her prison." At eight, she was deposited at an Augustinian convent against her will. "She remained there, as in a prison, for several years," insisting she would not willingly take vows that would exclude her from her rightful inheritance. When the day came, "she feigned herself sick and took to her bed. But this did not prevent her being carried to the church" by those who stood to benefit by her losing her inheritance. She was "blessed by a monk, in spite of her cries and protests." She escaped "without leave and returned to the world, which in heart she had never left." She married and in 1383, with the pope's consent, she was officially released from the order.[13]

Katie's escape was not quite so dramatic, and in the next two years, while living in Wittenberg, her trail grows dim. And why would anyone take particular notice of her? She is simply one of nine "wretched" nuns trying to make her way in the outside world, three having already gotten off the bus in Torgau. For a time, she lived in the home of Wittenberg's well-to-do city clerk. Here little is known of her, apart from a romance gone sour. The family with whom she lived had friends, the Baumgärtners, in Nuremberg, whose son Jerome had studied at the University of Wittenberg under Philip Melanchthon and Martin Luther. Jerome arrived back in town in the late spring of 1523 to visit with friends, including the family Katie was living with. Close in age—Jerome was a year older—they spent time together. Words were spoken, yea, more than words—sweet nothings and future plans for life together. He was expected back at his parents' home, but promised to return to Wittenberg soon.

There are serious biographers and ordinary wags who suggest that Katie was plain-looking, proud, and difficult to get along with. It would seem that Jerome clearly thought otherwise, or believed that such minor matters did not cancel out her otherwise fine attributes. He arrived back in Nuremberg to share his good news.

However, when Mom and Dad Baumgärtner learned of the plans, they were truly upset with their son's choice—a runaway nun without an estate or even enough money to support herself? Even at his age, the approval of parents was a requisite. So, did he travel back to Wittenberg to clarify the circumstances? Did he send her a compassionate and sensitive letter explaining how his hands were tied? Actually, Jerome was a cad. He did not even answer Katie's several letters. What could she do? Martin Luther to the rescue. A letter dated October 12, 1524. Prestigious professor and singular Reformer, his involvement would surely carry weight: "If you want your Katie von Bora, you had best act quickly, before she is given to someone else who wants her"[14]—as though eligible bachelors were lined up at her door. If jealousy would not stir Jerome, Luther turned to pity, saying she was brokenhearted and still in love with him. If not pity, surely the student should heed his distinguished professor, who would be most pleased by their marriage.

In the meantime, Katie had left the home of Jerome's family friends (who apparently did not intervene on her behalf) and moved to another home hardly beyond earshot in the town of Wittenberg. Here she would have been unaware that she was residing with a man who would become a famous artist, Lucas Cranach the Elder. Cranach was a wealthy nobleman, remembered today as a prominent sixteenth-century artist. But to the folks around Wittenberg, he was a town councilman, a three-term mayor, and the CEO of a prosperous art workshop attached to his large, remodeled home. Who knew his art would be widely displayed on the Internet a half millennium hence?

Around 1510, Cranach had married Barbara Brengbier, daughter of a distinguished mayor, and in the years that followed, she would give birth to two sons and three daughters—with Martin Luther agreeing to be godfather to both the oldest son and youngest daughter. Welcomed into the Cranach home, Katie was anything but idle, quickly plunging into housework and child care. At that time, the five children ranged in age from three to eleven.

Historian Steven Ozment extracts an interesting tale out of one of Cranach's works, painted shortly after Katie has become Frau Luther. The setting is a baptism:

> Thickly ringed around the baptismal pool are some of Wittenberg's most important women, there from the ranks of both the living and the dead. Mixed into the throng are the wives of the city's theologians and pastors: Katherine Luther and the late Barbara Cranach, the living Katherine Jonas and Walburga Bugenhagen.
>
> The most prominent, yet least seen, of those women is surprisingly Barbara Cranach (d. 1541). The viewer beholds only her imposing, centerfront backside clothed from neck to toe in the brocade and furs of a rich person. If local gossip is to be believed, she earned this anonymous cameo by repeatedly complaining that her husband had "never painted her." Whatever the truth of the story, her nagging seems to have [backfired]" because "her husband's blunt portrayal [of her] as a clothes-horse left her still not properly seen in a work of art, and thus not truly painted by her husband.[15]

How, we wonder, did Barbara treat Katie the impoverished nun? There is no evidence she was recommending her as a wife to their close friend Martin.

Had Luther previously been disingenuous in his claim to Jerome that there were others who wanted her? Might he have been referring to himself? Some have speculated as much. Indeed, Katie was a real catch. Although she "was not a regular beauty," according to James Anderson, "both Erasmus and [Jesuit] Maimbourg . . . eulogize her as possessed of . . . a dignity, without affectation, about her air and manner, which at the very first sight commanded respect."[16] From a letter written by an observer at the time, we learn that Luther "took a wife, from the noted Bora family, a girl of elegant appearance, 26 years old but poor."[17]

Exactly when Luther began contemplating getting married himself is not known. But in a letter to George Spalatin in the spring of 1525, he wrote, "Do not wonder that a famous lover like me does not marry. It is strange that I, who so frequently write about matrimony and get mixed up with women, have not yet turned into a woman, to say nothing of having married one." He jokes about losing two potential "wives" to others. "The third I can hardly hold on to with my left arm, and she too may soon be snatched away."[18]

All this time, there had been no word from Jerome. Were the Wittenbergers surprised when news came some two years after he had jilted Katie that he was marrying the fresh and nubile valley girl Sibylle, fourteen, pretty, and rich? The breakup with Katie turned out to be his loss, her gain—though she still may have been in no mood to recognize it.

Luther's efforts to find Katie a husband had been aided by others, including his colleague Nicolaus von Amsdorf, who almost appears to have been auctioning her and other nuns off rather than simply arranging marriages. To Spalatin, he had recommended "the best-born among them," sister of his uncle Dr. Staupitz, whom both he and Luther regarded very highly. "But," he continued, "if you wish to have a younger one, you shall have your choice of the fairest of them."[19]

With help from others, Luther had successfully found husbands for the nuns who desired marriage—all except for Katie. In his mind, after the Jerome debacle, any good Christian man would do, even the elderly pastor Casper Glatz. But Katie was not about to be pushed into the arms of a man for whom she had no affection, no doubt still pining for the man she loved. When Amsdorf had earlier written for financial support from Spalatin, he had commended the poor nuns with "neither shoes nor clothes" as "fair, fine, all of noble birth, and none of them is fifty years old."[20] Katie was in her mid-twenties, and she made it clear to Luther that the much older Casper was not suitable.

A marriage to Nicolaus Amsdorf, however, was a different matter. And so we move on to the next soap-opera episode in "As the World Turns." She considered him a suitable spouse and suggested as much to him, adding that if he were unwilling to take the plunge, she would be willing to consider Martin Luther himself—another old man, some sixteen years her senior. This is a stunning turn of events. If anyone previously had not recognized the true grit of this former nun, it would become glaringly obvious when she herself proposed marriage, not to one but two men, both renowned figures of the day. It was a bold move, and it worked.

At this point, the wheels are in motion. Had it been a hard sell on her part? Was she aware of his misgivings at the time? Did she ever learn that he married her out of pity? Years later, in 1538, he reportedly boasted that his first choice of a wife (thirteen years earlier) was not Katie, but Ave von Schönfeld, who had been snatched up by a Prussian physician. But when Katie was left with no other suitable prospects for a husband, he agreed to marry her out of pity. Though she was arrogant and proud, he soon realized she was a most reliable wife.[21]

Although he may have married Katie out of pity, Luther was prompted to take a wife for other reasons, as he colorfully confessed: to "please his father, rile the pope, make the angels laugh and the devils weep, and would seal his testimony."[22] And he was strongly encouraged by friends as well, including his ardent supporter Argula von Grumbach, who was convinced that his marrying would dispel scandalous rumors. But Luther was reticent, as he wrote to George Spalatin late in 1524:

I thank Argula for what she writes me concerning my marrying. I do not wonder at such gossip, for all sorts of reports are circulated about me. Thank her in my name, and tell her I am in God's hands, a creature whose heart he is able to change and change again, to kill and make alive every hour and moment. But so long as I am in my present mood I shall not marry. Not that I do not feel my sex, for my heart is neither wood nor stone; but my inclination is against marriage, for I am in daily expectation of death and of punishment suited to a heretic.[23]

Although little is known about Katharina during the years between 1523, when she escaped the convent, and 1525, when she married Luther, those years, however, were anything but blank. Part of this time was taken up with a roller-coaster ride of emotions. Many of us know what it's like to wait for letters in the mail and then to be jilted by someone we love—perhaps even someone we know simply isn't right for us. We can feel the raw betrayal, and we want to reach back in time and put our arms around her.

We wince when we imagine how difficult it was to be wearing cast-off gowns and worn-out shoes while living in the fancy Cranach household. Was the lady of the house haughty and critical, shameless in her costly brocade gowns? How we wish we had a journal entry in which Katharina poured out her heart. We want to know how she felt when she realized she was essentially being auctioned off as a bride, maybe to some schlep whose ministerial credentials did not make up for what was lacking in a potential husband. Did she cringe when she heard jokes and snide remarks at the expense of the *alte Jungfer*, an "old maid," "on the shelf," "spinster"? And then there is that notion that even before she escaped, she had her eye on marrying the great Reformer.

I'm reminded of my freshman year at a Bible college in the mid-1960s when most of the young women students were accused of enrolling for the purpose of earning their MRS degree. Sure we laughed, but I knew instinctively it was a pejorative term, derogatory of women.

Now when I contemplate Katie, I occasionally come across that same MRS-degree mentality. "Personally," writes Glenn Sunshine, "I suspect she was looking to marry Luther from before she left the convent."[24]

Such speculation is condescending. Katie was a cloistered and protected nun whose midnight escape was focused on freedom—and safety. Her destination was a scary world of rapid change and revolution. Even today, the relocation of a nun from an insular convent to a life on the outside involves culture shock. How different daily life was in the sixteenth century when a nun escaping a convent was committing a serious crime. That she would have pined for Martin Luther, who was himself running from the law, does not square with what must have been going through her mind as she and the other nuns planned their getaway. They were not bent on graduating with an MRS degree.

Also denigrating is the repeated suggestion that Katie was not a pretty young woman, as Preserved Smith and others have emphasized. "The portrait of Katie," writes Smith, "does not bear out the conjecture of Erasmus that the monk had been led astray by a wonderfully charming girl (*mire venusta*)."[25] Smith, at a centuries-long distance, judged her to be homely:

> She was of a type not uncommon among Germans, in whose features shrewdness, good sense, and kindliness often give a pleasant expression to homely persons—though even this can hardly be seen in Cranach's picture. Her scant reddish hair is combed back over a high forehead; the brows over her dark blue eyes slant up from a rather flat nose; her ears and cheek-bones are prominent.[26]

Obviously, beauty is in the eye of the beholder. I look at the same Cranach portrait and wonder about the artist himself. And of course his portrait of Martin does not exactly show the man to be a handsome stud. Enough about Katie's looks. To his credit, Smith goes on to at least partially redeem himself—on a matter far more significant than looks: "Katie was sometimes reproached with pride and avarice. But that an orphan, without friends, money, or beauty should have any pride left is rather a subject for praise than blame."[27]

Although Luther may have implied as late as 1525 that she had suitors, she did not. By any standard, she was spirited, energetic, competent, and a real catch, but her options were slim: Amsdorf or Luther. In the end, it was Luther who showed up at the Cranach home to arrange to take her as his wife and to get it over with as soon as possible. She was not so naive as to realize that his decision was not for love—and perhaps neither was hers.

If we were sitting at table with Luther's colleagues three days after the marriage, we might turn to Philip Melanchthon. Why, we would ask him, did his close friend make this sudden decision? His thoughts are written in a letter to Joachim Camerarius:

> On June 13, Luther unexpectedly and without informing in advance any of his friends of what he was doing, married Bora . . .
>
> These things have occurred, I think, somewhat in this way: The man is certainly pliable; and the nuns have used their arts against him most successfully; thus probably society with the nuns have softened or even inflamed this noble and highspirited man. In this way he seems to have fallen into this untimely change of life. The rumor, however, that he had previously dishonored her is manifestly a lie . . . I have hopes that this state of life may sober him down, so that he will discard the low buffoonery which we have often censured.[28]

We sum up his remarks: Bora used her magical arts to inflame a noble man, snare him as husband, sober him up, and rid him of low buffoonery. Good enough reasons for the great Reformer to marry.

Luther's upcoming marriage would rightly be hailed as a profound landmark in Reformation progress. But it was by no means the first. As the Lutheran theologian Justus Jonas observed, it was Bartholomäus

Bernhardi's public marriage in 1521, soon after the Diet of Worms, that led to "many thousand priests and monks deciding to marry."[29] Bernhardi was a fervent supporter of Luther, having been a student at Wittenberg. Not until 1523, however, did the matrimonial flood actually begin. By the end of that year, nearly one hundred priests, monks, and nuns had publicly tied the knot, most of them with no direct connection to Luther or to Wittenberg. Other clerics before this had married, but rarely in a public celebration.

Nevertheless, the significance of Martin Luther's marriage would be difficult to exaggerate. On the same day that Melanchthon wrote his letter about Luther having "fallen into this untimely change of life," Luther wrote to his friend Spalatin, "I have stopped the mouths of my calumniators with Catherine von Bora . . . I have made myself so cheap and despised by this marriage that I expect the angels laugh and the devils weep thereat."[30]

Did Katie realize the profound significance of her marriage? There is no evidence she did. She had escaped the convent with no specific future plan, and two years later, she found herself to be the last nun standing. Luther was one of two she would accept, having been jilted by the man she truly loved.

A footnote to Katie's two years of trial before she married relates to Jerome, the cad who did not even have the decency to officially break off their relationship. Martin had given him a pass because his first responsibility was to honor his parents. Their fierce opposition to their son marrying a destitute runaway nun apparently trumped any kindness he should have shown to her. In succeeding years, Martin had contact with his former student on other matters, and on one occasion he added to a letter a comment that he was sending friendly greetings from Katie, "his old flame."[31] Among her other positive qualities, Katharina von Bora had class.

CHAPTER

"A Bitter Living"

DAILY LIFE in OLD WITTENBERG

Lost in the annals of time and for all practical purposes nameless, she was a self-described "poor woman with only a small field," forced to "earn a bitter living."[1] Her lot in life was typical of many, if not most, women in early modern Germany, and not just widows. Most families were poor, whether they were numbered among the peasants or artisans. If the husband was old or infirm, the responsibility of breadwinner was relegated to the wife. This would be essentially true of the widowed Katharina, though before Martin died, she enjoyed a comparably comfortable lifestyle. But all around her were women who were barely eking out "a bitter living."

I grew up poor. My first memories are of a barely insulated farmhouse, no electricity, no indoor plumbing, my earliest education in a one-room schoolhouse. When the bus stalled in a deep snowdrift, I remember my father arriving with a team of horses to take the driver and children home, all of us bundled under blankets. In some ways, I can relate to the daily life of the sixteenth century more easily than colleagues who grew up in affluent homes in East Grand Rapids. I can hear the horses and feel the deep ruts as Katie and her sister nuns bumped along in the night toward Torgau.

But with all the hardships I encountered as a child, we would have never used the phrase "bitter living." Nor was Katie's life a bitter living, at least until her last years when the ravages of war, weather, and physical injuries took their toll. For most families, however, living in the small towns and backwoods of what is now Germany, life was grim—more so for women whose workdays extended from dawn until well after dark. Modern conveniences were available if you were a member of the royalty or otherwise rich. But for the rest of the population, housework was drudgery, and hiring a servant was not financially feasible. Even a decent outhouse was not a standard amenity.

"In Ancient Egypt rich people had proper bathrooms and toilets in their homes," writes Tim Lambert. As we move ahead in history, however, we see serious toilet regression. "In the Middle Ages toilets were simply pits in the ground with wooden seats over them."[2]

By the time I was born in rural northern Wisconsin, farm families had long ago progressed enough to put a little house over a hole in the ground to conceal a bench with a rounded opening (sometimes two), leaving enough space for a Sears & Roebuck catalog (far superior than the leaves of the woolly mullein plant used by medievals). Lambert writes, "In Medieval castles the toilet was called a garderobe and it was simply a vertical shaft with a stone seat at the top. Some garderobes emptied into the moat."[3]

The facilities in convents and monasteries were often comparable to those in castles. Sometimes "monks built stone or wooden lavatories over rivers."[4] Some plumbing systems were even more sophisticated: "At Portchester Castle in the 12th century monks built stone chutes leading to the sea. When the tide went in and out it would flush away the sewage."[5] Katie would have been used to more than simply a hole in the ground, and when she joined Martin at the Black Cloister, plumbing would have been comparable to that of other run-down cloisters of the day.

Life was rugged in this era—especially in a one-time backwater village like Wittenberg. Modern-day Wittenberg welcomes guests to a quaint, cleaned-up tourist town. It is charming, warm, and hospitable to travelers. TripAdvisor lists the ten best restaurants, all brand-new since 1517—actually, new since East Germany opened up to the West in 1989. Another site lists the top ten hotels. As much as we long to visit actual historic sites, we know very well what five hundred years can do to a little town known for its larger-than-life Reformer. If Martin Luther had never nailed or taught or settled down in that town, we might find it today trashier than it was when he lived there.

What was daily life like after Katie arrived in Wittenberg with eight other runaway nuns? She had the good fortune of being housed most of the time in mansions, at least by local standards. And she quickly came to know the little hamlet, including fields, woods, and streams nearby. Writers of the day variously described the town in the 1520s. The problem is that, like hometown folks and outsiders today, they write with an agenda, though perhaps less so Philip Melanchthon, who referred to Wittenberg as no more than a village comprised of mud huts with thatched roofs and lopsided houses, with no evidence of pride or city planning.[6] That he was a university-educated humanist who had resided in actual cities, may have influenced his rather negative assessment, but he had no particular axe to grind or reason to comically disparage the town.

Not so Luther, who is quoted as saying, "Here in Wittenberg there's no more than a miserable corpse; we sit here in Wittenberg as if it were a miserable place."[7] His droll exaggeration was no doubt influenced by one of his bad days. But Wittenberg, even on its best days after it had come out of its long night of medieval lassitude, was not a village we could today endure without some serious sanitary codes. Roland Bainton's description would fit almost any sixteenth-century town. Larger cities were no doubt even worse:

> There is no denying that he [Luther] was not fastidious, nor was his generation. Life itself stank. One could not walk around Wittenberg without encountering the odors of the pigsty, offal, and the slaughterhouse. And even the most genteel were not reticent about the facts of daily experience. Katie, when asked about the congregation on a day when Luther was unable to

attend, replied, "The church was so full it stank." "Yes," said
Luther, "they had manure on their boots."[8]

One of Luther's enemies belittled the town nearly as much as did the
Reformer himself, calling it a "miserable, filthy little town" that pales in
comparison to Prague. It was no more than "a peasants' chamber; rough;
half-frozen; joyless; filled with muck."[9] How could such a miserable
hamlet even imagine itself challenging the authority of Rome?

An objective assessment of sixteenth-century Wittenberg is
impossible, but it did have some favorable qualities. It was a fortified
town with stone walls, giving it a look of substance, however small, with
a moat surrounding the walls. In 1485, when Frederick III the Wise
succeeded his father, he made Wittenberg the capital of his electorate
and then founded a university in 1502. This fortified town boasted
not only a mill but also water power, a major engineering project
completed some generations earlier. Indeed, it was an unusual scene
to have two fast-flowing streams cutting right through town. There
was danger as well, when carousing, beer-drinking students staggered
toward campus late at night.[10]

Indeed, Wittenberg was a college town, with all the rowdiness that
comes with late-night reveling. There was beer aplenty—also prostitutes—to keep restless students jolly. Luther was not amused by such
behavior, associating it with low morals perpetuated by the Catholic
Church, certainly not by Reformers. He was well aware that what he
was hearing was more than rumor of boastful exploits—that, in fact,
students at his own university were seeking the services of prostitutes,
who plied their trade "in the vicinity of the town's pig-market." Luther
was quick with his pen. The essay was titled "Against the Whores and
Fat-Students."[11]

At the turn of the century, when word spread of the plans for
Frederick's new university, the town quickly increased the number of
dwellings. And as early as 1504, local councilmen had written a new
code to provide for student housing, specifying that anyone who had

a vacant lot was required to construct a home within a year.[12] In early 1521, the student body—male only—approached three thousand, with more students than town residents. Many of them had come to sit at the feet of Martin Luther, although there were other professors, including Philip Melanchthon, whose reputation rivaled that of the great Reformer.

By the time Katie arrived in 1523, however, the student enrollment had fallen off. Fear for their lives due to the Edict of Worms and Luther's hiatus at the Wartburg Castle contributed to a decrease. Still students would have been the most visible presence of the town population. Katie might have been aware of them mocking her and the eight other "wretched" nuns who clumsily hoisted themselves off the wagon, and she might not have appreciated being identified as one among the virgins who had just come to town. Runaway nuns certainly would have been fodder for jest, whether the students were drinking or not.

As capable as Katie was, it is doubtful that she ever even thought about gender and privilege and lack of higher education for women. She was no doubt fully aware, however, of the Renaissance assumption that boys deserved a good education. "A father who does not arrange for his son to receive the best education at the earliest age," wrote Erasmus, "is neither a man himself nor has any fellowship with human nature."[13] And what about daughters? Her future husband would see to it that progress was made in that direction.

The growth of the university exposed the shortage of housing for professors. As is true today, it is difficult for a school of higher learning to attract distinguished professors unless the available housing is fitting of their prestige. Gottfried Krüger's assessment of Wittenberg before and during Katie's residence makes us believe that on settling in, she must have been impressed. Despite the negative press, Wittenberg by the 1520s was in many ways a respectable college town, no longer a two-bit hamlet unworthy of recognition.[14]

Wittenberg, like all towns of the day, offered inns for travelers. They were typically dirty, smelly, disease-ridden, cramped houses, not to be confused with the more spacious, well-kept Black Cloister boardinghouse where Katie served as matron during her twenty-year marriage and on into widowhood. A travel writer in early sixteenth-century Germany offers a glimpse of typical accommodations—a country inn "no worse than most inns in a German land." There was no custom of welcoming guests. "Upon arrival, we initiate the ritual necessary to secure a bed," he writes. "We stand out in the yard for an interminable time and yell. God forbid that the innkeeper should greet us, for we Germans consider it demeaning to trawl for paying guests." Finally someone's "head thrusts forward from a tiny window and you inquire about lodging. If they have none, they say so. But if they do, they don't answer your question, but simply withdraw, to meander out a little later, feigning indifference."[15]

There was no one to water and feed the horses, so the guests had to do that themselves and "then enter the common room, which is indeed common, as all guests are here, in their boots, with their baggage and road dust. There must be eighty or ninety people." Some of the wayfarers are "decidedly ill, but these are housed with the rest of us. Men, women, children, rich and poor, sick or well, all share the same fetid air, for Germans consider it the height of hospitality to warm their guests to a lather." The place stank to high heaven, "not a man present whose clothes are not dark with sweat." Yet when this traveler's companion "dares open the window a little, a terrible clamor of indignation is heard."[16] So they settled down amid grunts and snores, rasping coughs and vomiting—just another night on the road.

Wittenberg during the early decades of the sixteenth century is best understood as a growing center of scholarship, court activities, and commerce. Despite a temporary drop in student population by the 1520s, the town was becoming a bustling urban hub, particularly in comparison to its long night as a medieval backwater. Preserved Smith offers an overview of the rapid changes that were taking place:

> Wittenberg lies along the inner curve of the winding, eddy-
> ing Elbe, in the midst of a sandy plain neither fertile nor beautiful.

Frequent floods and poor drainage made the town unwholesome. Prior to the close of the fifteenth century it was a mere hamlet, with about three hundred and fifty low, ugly, wooden houses and few public buildings . . . Frederic the Wise, anxious to build up a capital equal to Leipsic, adorned the town with a new church and a university. The rise of the Evangelic teaching made Wittenberg one of the capitals of Europe, and its growth and improvement kept pace with its more exalted position.[17]

If any of the many students in town had paid heed to the runaway nun Katharina once she had settled down, they did not make note of it. She would have been easily overlooked as she hurried through the market or stopped by a shop for shoe repair. Though for a time she lived in the largest and most elaborate house in town owned by artist Lucas Cranach, she was probably regarded as little more than a servant. Her everyday attire would likely have been coarse and plain.

Long skirts were standard for all women, sometimes partially pulled up and tied to a belt when working in the privacy of an isolated backyard garden. Panties were not standard, making it easier for a full-throttled thug to savagely assault and rape an unsuspecting woman. Covering of the head (or braiding hair for girls) was not only a sign of submission but also a sign that a woman was appropriately clothed, never to be mistaken for a prostitute. In the winter a cape was added to the outfit. For women like Katie, a belt with a leather bag containing money and other small items was an essential accessory when running errands about town. Brightly colored fabric was typically the province of wealthy matrons.

Indeed, for wealthy perfumed Renaissance women, dresses, shoes, wigs, and jewelry were works of art in themselves. But when we visit sixteenth-century Germany, lower-class women would often be considered old hags by the time they are thirty. "Pre-industrial women—daughters, maidservants, wives, widows, and independent spinsters," writes Sheilagh Ogilvie, "appear again and again in local documents as responsible for their own subsistence, as earning 'a bitter living.'"[18]

It might be natural to assume that women in this era married early, endured childbirths, and died young, having spent fourteen-hour shifts of household drudgery year after year. But Ogilvie maintains that such was not always the case especially in northern and western Europe, "where marriage was late, lifetime celibacy was high, life-cycle service was widespread, and there were many female lodgers. Women were able to inherit land, were sent to school and were allowed to participate in labour markets."[19] Although this overview is based on research in the era soon after Katharina's death, its beginnings can be seen in her own life—in her insistence that she remain single rather than marry a man she did not esteem and also in her independent demeanor after her marriage. In pre-industrial German towns, "women could work outside the household as maidservants or even independent employees, earning wages at tasks that were not constrained by reproductive activities."[20]

Marriage and reproductive activities, however, would soon constrain Katie. Statistics tell us that childbirth for both mother and child was perilous during this era, and plagues swept through cities, small towns, and the countryside at regular intervals. Joel Harrington points out that life was precarious even before an infant was born with an estimated one in three pregnancies not coming to term. The odds were even as to whether or not a child would live to age twelve. "The first two years of a child's life were the most dangerous," according to Harrington, due to "frequent outbreaks of smallpox, typhus, and dysentery [that] proved particularly fatal to younger victims."[21]

Adding to the very real scourges and maladies and significant problems of early medical malpractice were superstitions that might have easily kept a mother and wife like Katie awake at night. Horror stories of unexplained happenings were everywhere in the air, and not just among the lower classes but among the brightest and best of Wittenberg. Kaspar Peucer, son-in-law of Philip Melanchthon, researched such phenomenon and published his findings in *Commentary on the Various Types of Divinations*. Here he presented all manner of unexplained marvels, including a 1531 multiple birth in Augsburg:

"three offspring, one a head wrapped in membranes, the second a serpent with two legs, the body and the feet of a toad, and the tail of a lizard, the third a perfectly normal pig."[22]

Why would a rational sixteenth-century philosopher and theologian such as Peucer, and others like him, make such claims? Euan Cameron, in his book *Enchanted Europe*, has sought to explain:

> They confronted the brutal facts that children fell sick and died; that cows mysteriously failed to give milk; that horses either bolted or suffered from unexplained exhaustion; that summer storms came from nowhere to devastate the crops; and that less educated people persisted in believing in the existence of a huge, amorphous variety of semi-visible or invisible spirit-creatures who might influence their lives. Ecclesiastical authors struggled to make sense of these mysteries and, even more, to analyse the exotic variety of remedies and prophylaxes that people traditionally used against them. The superstition-critique presents pastoral theology at its most practical, specific, and applied. Moreover, since pastoral theologians participated in the broad culture of their birth as much as in the formal intellectual habits of their professional training, the analysis of "superstition" challenged them repeatedly to navigate their own way between custom and instinct on one hand and intellectual formation on the other. Occasionally . . . the mask slipped. Sometimes it fell away altogether.[23]

Katie does not seem to have been susceptible to such superstitious fears. Her world was all too real, and her worries were reality based. Perhaps her years in the convent had focused her attention on a fear of God more than sinister spirits in the surrounding dark forests. But the convent also offered women other health benefits. For celibate nuns, childbirth was not a killer. Nor were long days of backbreaking toil. And contagious diseases sometimes passed right over the rooftops of isolated convents. The very isolation, however, held horrifying dangers as well. Convents were often easy targets for barbarian thugs. Despite walls and moats, a nun who ventured alone into the garden might be attacked and dragged into the tangled forest. In fact, this was the very crime Catholics alleged had taken place when Leonard Koppe kidnapped Katie and her sister nuns from the Marienthron convent.

Crimes of all kinds were rife throughout the Middle Ages, and the lawlessness continued without abatement into sixteenth-century Germany. And not just one boorish hooligan acting alone. Warring militias and marauding bandits could overrun towns and leave in their path only charred remains. Indeed, the fear of the torch was one of the most terrifying features of life during this era. Mutilated bodies were left along roads to be fought over by buzzards. Mayhem was everywhere in this era when forensic science was unknown and crime investigation depended largely on eyewitness accounts. Serious crimes often went unpunished, while the innocent were found guilty. Penalties were severe.

Katie would have been well aware of how punishment for a capital crime was meted out. "A woodcut of 1540, attributed to Lucas Cranach the Younger," writes C. Scott Dixon, "depicts the charred remains of four criminals, each bound to a stake, with the slightly altered text of Romans 13:4 . . . 'The sovereign powers are not to be feared by those who do good, but rather by those who do ill.'" Dixon goes on to suggest that Luther, "by limiting the powers of Christ's kingdom to purely spiritual concerns," granted "an unprecedented strength of rule to the early modern state."[24]

"While John Calvin remained content to acknowledge the executioner as 'God's instrument,'" writes Joel Harrington, "the ever-ebullient Luther went so far as to provide a celebrity endorsement for the profession: 'If you see that there is a lack of hangmen . . . and you find that you are qualified, you should offer your services and seek the position so that the essential governmental authority may not be despised or become enfeebled.'"[25]

Crime was seemingly everywhere in sixteenth-century Germany. This was particularly true for travelers, who were all too often robbed of their possessions and left for dead. Safety was found in numbers, and when he traveled, Martin Luther (unlike his wife) was often accompanied by others who simply enjoyed being in his company.

Harrington writes, "Well-traveled paths and country lanes often lay far from help as well. The roads and forests just outside a city, along with all border territories, were especially dangerous. There a traveler might fall prey to bandit gangs led by vicious outlaws such as Cunz Schott, who not only beat and robbed countless victims, but also made a point of collecting the hands of citizens from his self-declared enemy, Nuremberg."[26]

In addition to very real bandits, some known by name, there were other forces at work that scared the living daylights out of travelers: "Hostile natural and supernatural forces, mysterious and deadly epidemics, violent and malevolent fellow human beings, accidental or intentional fires—all haunted the imaginations and daily lives of early modern people."[27]

Emperor Maximilian I more or less conceded the violent chaos that prevailed throughout his realm, proclaiming in his 1495 Perpetual Truce, "No one, whatever his rank, estate, or position, shall conduct feud, make war on, rob, kidnap, or besiege another . . . nor shall he enter any castle town, market, fortress, villages, hamlets, or farms against another's will, or use force against them; illegally occupying them, threaten them with arson, or damage them in any other way."[28]

It was a truce aimed in the right direction, but it probably had no more force than a church mission statement would have today. Its significance lies in its description of daily life.

Perhaps the most private crime of the era was abortion and infanticide. The Luthers themselves were involved in a situation that illustrates a behind-the-scenes attempt to induce an abortion. In a letter from Wittenberg to a judge in Leipsic, dated January 29, 1544, Martin informed his "good friend" that he had learned that a woman who identified herself as Rosina von Truchses was being housed as a guest. In truth, he said, the woman was a "shameful liar" with a false identity who had "played the harlot behind my back and foully deceived every one with the name Truchses."[29]

Having been fooled himself, Martin was now warning the judge: "I took her into my own house with my own children. She had lovers and became pregnant and asked one of my maids to jump on her body and kill the unborn child. She escaped through the compassion of my Katie; otherwise she would have deceived no more men unless the Elbe ran dry."[30]

What Luther would have done to prevent her from ever again deceiving men, he does not specify, though he ends his righteous rant with these words: "I fear that if a strict inquiry should be made, she would be found to deserve death more than once . . . I have written to [warn] . . . you against this damned, lying, thievish harlot."[31] This was no doubt a man's world and a violent time. It is also interesting to learn of the woman's escape with the help of Katie. What happened to the unborn child is unknown. Abortion and infanticide were often considered matters better relegated to the private world of women.

Sixteenth-century Wittenberg, and all of Europe for that matter, was a man's world. Though expected to remain faithful to his wife, the man had far greater sexual freedom than she, and even Protestant Zurich kept its brothel. Illicit sex was common among every social class. A dowry paid by the bride's family was a common practice among upper classes, causing parents to celebrate the birth of a boy. Failure of a wife to become pregnant was commonly blamed on the wife—or witchcraft. The husband, however, was sometimes mocked for his insufficient manliness. After all, it was widely believed that women had no part in conception except for providing the incubator for the male "seed."

It was during this era that the most primitive condoms were in use. Homemade or underground-manufactured linen pouches soaked in chemicals and then dried were the most effective available. Not until the mid-nineteenth century were rubber condoms available. But such forms of birth control were used only by adulterous husbands and young unmarried men. For married couples, children were highly prized.

From a young age, children were harshly disciplined and expected to work long days alongside their parents. Reformers and humanists, however, would emphasize education and children's participation in music and games. Luther loved to sing and play games with the children; Katie as well, when she had a free moment from her hectic schedule.

Mealtime was an important event for sixteenth-century Germans, and a meat casserole—or roasted meat—was the preferred entrée. In Wittenberg and elsewhere among the dense forests of Europe, wild game and birds were readily available. Fish offered a nutritious alternative, and, of course, bread and fresh vegetables from a well-tended garden made a hardy supper complete. Milk and beer were standard beverages, and a good meal might be topped off with *lebkuchen* or honey cakes.

For most women there was little time for relaxation. We might like to think of Katie in an easy chair, curled up with a book, but that would be highly unlikely. Not that such pastimes would have been unavailable to her. Growing up in the 1520s, Teresa of Ávila later confessed that as a girl she had succumbed to reading romance novels: "So excessively was I absorbed in it that I believe, unless I had a new book, I was never happy."[32] There were devotional books and handbooks on godly child rearing, but it is unlikely that the busy Katharina would have made time to read them.

Katie was, however, fully aware of books and tracts and was actively involved in the publishing and promotion of her husband's writing. Of the two of them, she was the one with business acumen. With the invention of the movable press, the book business had skyrocketed after the turn of the sixteenth century. Most of the pamphlets and books available were sold by book peddlers and, after that, the earliest version of the bookmobile, a donkey-driven covered wagon that made regular circuits from town to town.

If she had little or no time in her days left for reading, we might ask why she didn't at least take a few private moments every day for writing. After all, writing and especially publishing were the hottest activities of the day, and in the convent, Katie surely must have been aware of nuns who were writers. One sister from a convent in Brussels in the late fifteenth century had managed to steal enough time from her daily duties to write two pages a day. And Teresa of Ávila found time amid her travels and busy schedule to write her autobiography, *The Life of Teresa of Jesus*.

But women generally were discouraged from writing. "Many of those who chose to recall sixteenth-century female authors," writes Susan Broomhall, "praised women grudgingly, if at all." Of Marie de Gournay's writing, it was said, "She was familiar with all the learned languages; she wrote badly in her own; but it was a great deal then for a woman even to know how to write."[33]

One could hope that Marie was as proud and strong-minded as Katie was accused of being. There were many such women on the streets and byways of sixteenth-century Germany, and that was the only way to thrive in this very politically incorrect culture that regarded ridiculing women to be a sport. Katie pulled herself out of "a bitter living" by sheer determination and chutzpah. She stood her ground and sassed back, as did other women of the era.

In her book *Mothers and Daughters in Medieval German Literature*, Ann Marie Rasmussen tells stories of sixteenth-century women who "resorted to tactics of shame and public ridicule in order to enforce their claims." In one instance, "a seduced [or raped] maid servant . . . jumped up on her seducer's marriage cart and refused to get off until she had received payment."[34] The woman who was already the object of derision turned the tables on the offending man. This is just one example of female empowerment that was not entirely uncommon in the Reformation era.

Though never in such a brazen manner, Katie's self-confidence would also be on display for all to see. Old Wittenberg was a man's world, and in her own way, she would jump up on the marriage cart of male dominion and assert her rightful place.

"Pigtails on the Pillow"

MARRIAGE TO MARTIN LUTHER

Four days after his marriage to Katharina, Martin Luther sent word to Leonard Koppe that he had been "woven into the braids of his concubine."[1] Although Luther was apparently making jest, it was a strange statement in light of the fact that his enemies had been saying the very same thing—spreading rumors prior to the marriage that Luther was taking a nun to bed. To another friend Luther wrote, "Suddenly and while I was occupied with far other thoughts, the Lord has plunged me into marriage."[2] In both comments, he sees himself as passive, being acted on by others: *woven into* and *plunged into*. As he is telling the story, Katie and the Lord are responsible. No doubt, Luther was still somewhat insecure about his own marriage.

"Shotgun weddings becoming relics of another time" was a leading headline in *USA Today* (April 26, 2014). But when I was a young adult in the 1960s, such a quickly planned marriage was indeed a scandal—a scandal featuring a pregnant bride and an irate father, though probably not threatening the young man with an actual shotgun if he refused to marry his daughter.

Such a disgrace, however, would have paled in comparison to that seriously scandalous marriage in the summer of 1525. Indeed, starting a marriage amid a public uproar is not an ideal way to begin. Yet that is exactly how it was for Katie. Her husband was used to being in the thick of things, and a shocking marriage was only one of many slurs hurled against him since 1517. This situation, however, was different. He knew full well there would be serious censure even among his friends. "If I had not married quickly and secretly, and taken few into my confidence," he later wrote, "everyone would have done what he could to hinder me; for all my best friends cried: 'Not this one, but another.'"[3] That knowledge alone would have been enough to upset Katie, not to mention a public smear campaign that in hindsight was the sex scandal of the century (unless we are to include all the shame, corruption, and executions associated with the marriages of King Henry VIII).

It is difficult to comprehend the religious and social Zeitgeist of sixteenth-century Germany. We celebrate the five-hundred-year anniversary of 1517 and do our best to see the landscape as it was back then. But even the most gifted historians fall far short. Today the marriage of a monk and nun, both having left monasticism two or more years earlier, would hardly create a stir. What we would find most shocking about Martin and Katie's marriage would be the circumstances surrounding the consummation. Any secrecy prior to the marriage did not extend to the marriage bed itself. Indeed, what the bride and groom would normally want to be a very private occasion was anything but. Justus Jonas, Martin Luther's close friend, described the scene the following day: "I was present yesterday and saw the couple on their marriage bed. As I watched this spectacle I could not hold back my tears."[4] And what about Katie? How did she feel about this invasion of privacy? Had she been some sort of sixteenth-century floozy, it might have been different. I have long wondered whether Katie herself could hold back the tears during this "spectacle." It would be enough to make any bride weep.

Many have insisted that such was the practice of the day, not only for royal marriages, but in any instances when it was important to have proof that a marriage had been consummated. Patrick O'Hare (writing in 1916), one of Luther's harshest critics, however, blamed Luther, not custom, for "the vulgarity to lift the covers of the nuptial bed and disclose its sacred secrets to the gaze of others."[5] Such claims more than three centuries after the fact lose their sting. But at the time, the humiliating accusations were no doubt very hurtful.

Luther had expected to be censured, especially in his marriage to a nun. After all, he had been the howling critic only a few years earlier. "Good Heavens!" he wailed in a letter to George Spalatin, "will our Wittenbergers give wives even to the monks?" adding, "They won't force one on me."[6] Now, with what appeared to be undue eagerness to take a wife, he symbolized to some the depths of immorality that had been predicted. His marriage, they said, proved his reform was underwritten by the devil.

But why did he keep his marriage a secret from even his closest associates? His enemies had a swift response: he had already taken her to bed; she was already pregnant. Would the antichrist be born of such a union? And weren't they saying this nun would probably give birth to a pig or a toad? Rumors were flying. And not just about the two of them. What about his parents?

Where would such questions and claims come from? From uneducated backwoods peasants brimming with superstitious stories? Perhaps. But Johannes Cochlaeus, a university-educated Latin scholar, was the author of the influential and scurrilous *Commentary . . . on the Acts and Writings of Martin Luther*. Here he asserted that Luther's utter impiety resulted from his parentage—his father guilty of murder, his mother of selling herself for sex. Added to that, his father was actually not Hans, but a demonic spirit, an incubus.[7]

King Henry VIII, supreme head of the Church of England, also joined the chorus of criticism. Henry, of all people. He had not yet had his first and fourth marriages annulled, nor his second and fifth wives executed. His reputation was still intact when he contrasted the holy lives of the church fathers with the dissolute life of Luther. Then in 1527, he sponsored a stage play mocking the marriage of the monk and nun—a monastic brother and convent sister committing incest.[8]

Thomas More, who would be appointed Henry's lord chancellor in 1529 (only to be executed at the king's bidding in 1532) pointed a similarly sharp quill at the Reformer, as Catholic hatred of Luther was most creatively exemplified in More's writings, who, according to Helen L. Parish, "took evident delight in the polemical capital afforded by his opponent's personal life." He accused the Reformer of foul and fleshly sexual intercourse—even incest, because as a brother monk he had taken a sister nun to bed.[9]

Once Luther had made up his mind to marry, however, there was no reason why he should delay. Katie was the only escaped nun remaining, and she had let it be known that Martin would be a suitable husband for her. He had certainly realized by this time that she would be a competent and faithful wife. It was a marriage of partnership and convenience for both of them. Katie entered marriage, as did Martin, without heart-pounding passion. She believed he would make an acceptable husband, though theirs was hardly a flaming romance such as that with the man who had broken her heart.[10] For Luther's part, he later wrote, "I never loved Katie then for I suspected her of being proud (as she is), but God willed me to take pity on the poor abandoned girl."[11]

That Luther would be denounced by Catholic critics was to be expected, but he seemed to be surprised that many of his fellow Reformers were also upset and shell-shocked. In self-defense, he wrote:

> The report is true that I suddenly married Katherine to silence the mouths which are accustomed to bicker at me. I hope to live a short while yet, to gratify my father, who asked me to marry and leave him descendants. Moreover, I would confirm what I have taught by my example, for many are still afraid even in the present great light of the gospel. God has willed and caused my act, for I neither love my wife nor burn for her, but esteem her highly.[12]

God has willed and caused my act. Though Martin and Katie's was no shotgun marriage, the timetable had all the earmarks of such. Indeed, he followed his own advice "that the marriage be proclaimed publicly in the church and physically consummated as soon as possible."[13] His concern was to beat the censors: "For it is very dangerous to put off the marriage too long since Satan loves to erect obstacles and cause trouble through evil tongues, slanders, and the friends of both parties." The last phrase is interesting, the implication being that Katie, as well as Martin, may have had friends who objected to the union. It is well known that there were those on his side who, as he said, "would certainly have prevented it."[14]

So without wasting time, Martin walked over to the Cranach home, as he was often accustomed to doing. This time, however, he implemented the most important decision of his life. In effect, he was accepting the marriage proposal Katie had already made through Nicolaus von Amsdorf. He and Katie had a serious discussion, and the matter was settled. There is no evidence they had ever had a truly personal talk before this. As open as Luther was about private matters in his letters to friends, these moments are never described. We certainly hope he did not so much as hint to her that he was "showing mercy to the abandoned girl." However, we would be letting our imaginations get away from us if we pictured him taking her in his arms and passionately whispering her name. And how did she respond to the marriage proposal? *Well, okay, if that's what you want?* It was not an instantaneous proposal made in a haymow, but sex would come soon enough.

The marriage ceremony was what would have been considered irregular by sixteenth-century standards—and by Luther's own standard. It was a Tuesday evening, June 13, 1525, the setting the Augustinian Black Cloister (now Luther's home). There had been no prior announcement of the banns; rather, the engagement was made legal and was immediately followed by the marriage ceremony. Without further ado, the newlyweds went to their bed, accompanied by witnesses. Justus Jonas served as scribe, ready to share the news that he had seen his best friend having sex with his bride. The whole ordeal—from engagement to crawling out of bed—was probably wrapped up in less than a half hour. And hopefully, for the sake of Katie and the witnesses, the bed wasn't the same one described by Luther: "Before I was married the bed was not made for a whole year and became foul with sweat."[15]

Why, we wonder, did Luther add this addendum to his marriage ceremony? It is doubtful, as some have suggested, that this was an ancient German custom and a necessary requisite. More likely, Luther wanted the proof of consummation to be heralded abroad. He had said, perhaps offhandedly, less than two weeks earlier that he thought it might be God's will that he marry—even if it were only a *Joseph marriage*.[16] Catholic belief, of course, was that the marriage of the betrothed Mary and Joseph had never been consummated. Might Luther, after suggesting otherwise, have wanted it to be known that his was not a "Joseph marriage"?

Perhaps Martin remembered hearing a story told by Saint Gregory of Tours, a sixth-century bishop, whose ideal of marriage was one of celibacy. He related how the groom was with his bride in the bed chamber when she began weeping. When he asked what was wrong, she responded, "I had determined to preserve my poor body for Christ, untouched by intercourse with man . . . At the moment when . . . I should have put on the stole of purity, this wedding-gown brings me shame instead of honour." Though shocked by the news, the husband yielded to her desire: "If you are determined to abstain from intercourse with me, then I will agree to what you want to do." Then Gregory's punch line: "Hand in hand they went to sleep," thus living out the bishop's model for marriage. "And for many years after this they lay each night in one bed, but they remained chaste in a way which we can only admire."[17]

Luther made it crystal clear that wasn't the kind of marriage he was entering, and he had proof positive. His close friend and colleague Philip Melanchthon, however, was impressed with neither the marriage to Katie nor the proof of consummation. Luther knew as much and invited him neither to the private engagement and marriage nor to the public celebration. Suspecting Luther had married only for lust, Melanchthon lamented that "at this unfortunate time, when good and excellent men everywhere are in distress, he not only should be incapable of sympathizing with them, but should seem entirely careless concerning the evils everywhere abounding, and of diminishing his reputation just when Germany has especial need of his sound judgment and good name."[18]

The explosion of invective must have convinced Melanchthon he had been right. Luther's powerful opponent Duke George railed that the monk and nun were making a feast out of illicit sex.[19] And Luther's example was being repeated in all the monasteries in the land. The rumor mills were in overdrive. It was said that when they heard the wedding bells, "the lecherous monks and nuns put up plenty of ladders against the monastery walls and ran off together in masses."[20]

The wedding bells signaling the public ceremony rang at 10:00 a.m. on June 27. Martin and Katie walked to the church with family and friends, many having traveled from out of town. Accompanied by pipers and well-wishers, it was a grand celebration. When the short service was over the couple and their guests returned for dinner at the Black Cloister. Friends at Martin's request had brought beer and wild game. Festive dancing at the town hall followed, and then a banquet in the evening. It was a long day, and the couple was no doubt relieved when the last guests were gone.

On the guest list were Martin's family and friends, including his elderly mother and father, Margarethe and Hans Luther. To John von Dolzig, Luther had written:

> The strange cry, no doubt, has reached your ears, with regard to my having been married. And although this is rather a curious piece of news to me, and I can scarcely credit it myself, the testimony of the witnesses, nevertheless, is so overpowering, that I must out of becoming respect for them, give credit to it, and accordingly intend, on next Tuesday, with my father and mother and other friends, to seal and to confirm it by a collation. I therefore respectfully pray you, if it be not inconvenient, kindly

to provide me with some wild game, and to be present yourself, and, augmenting our joy, help to impress the seal, and the like.[21]

If Katie thought that the criticism and derision would now fade away, she was wrong. It continued not just in whispers but also in public outcries. In many people's eyes, she would always be the runaway nun who had forsaken her vows. Indeed, soon after they were married, a Wittenberg councilman's wife, Klara Eberhard, was summoned to court because "she spoke idle words, insulted, and told off Luther and Katie at a wedding." She was fined, but the damage had already been done.[22]

A widely circulated pamphlet summed up Katie's sins: "Woe to you, poor fallen woman" and your "damnable, shameful life." You arrived in Wittenberg dressed like a "chorus girl," living in sin with Luther, "forsaking Christ," and breaking your vows. "And by your example, have reduced many godly young women . . . to a pitiable state."[23]

Such personal polemics in print must have caused Katie to cringe, and it is doubtful she ever got used to it. An even greater adjustment would have been learning to live with her loutish husband. He admitted to not loving her in the early stages of their marriage, and it is not hard to imagine that his coarse language was often cutting. Sure, she was strong and confident, but there is no reason to believe she wasn't sensitive to less-than-loving words and ill-mannered body language.

Did she ever wonder if her marriage would even last? It was not to be assumed that nuns who tied the knot soon after leaving the convent automatically enjoyed fulfilling marriages. Many nuns who fled their cloistered lives remained single; some married and then separated from or were abandoned by their husbands. When several dozen cloistered nuns of St. Katharina faced harassment under Ulrich Zwingli's reform in Zurich, only three renounced their vows and one was quickly married, but some time later, she escaped from her husband and was taken in by a convent in Kreuzlingen.[24]

Another matter that may have troubled Katie was that of sexual intercourse. *What did she know and when did she know it?* the investigative historian asks. She might have received some pointers from Barbara Brengbier, wife of Lucas Cranach, in whose house she had lived, except for the fact that there was so little time between the surprise marriage proposal and wedding. We should not assume, however, that nuns were entirely in the dark about such matters. In fact, it is possible that she had read the words of another German nun who had written her *Liber subtilatum* nearly four centuries earlier. Indeed, one of Hildegard's strangest writings relates to women, sex, and how babies are conceived:

> When a woman is making love with a man, a sense of heat in her brain, which brings with it sensual delight, communicates the taste of that delight during the act and summons forth the emission of the man's seed. And when the seed has fallen into its place, that vehement heat descending from her brain draws the seed to itself and holds it, and soon the woman's sexual organs contract, and all the parts that are ready to open up during the time of menstruation now close, in the same way as a strong man can hold something enclosed in his fist.[25]

Whatever sex education Katie might have received at the convent, it no doubt paled in comparison to the work of housekeeping and gardening. The fields and woodlands owned by the Marienthron cloister included a number of properties that had been deeded to the convent. Two of the outlying farms were suitable for extensive sheepherding requiring dozens of farmhands. Such agricultural operations provided meat and grain for the nuns. Small-scale farming and gardening within the walls gave the community a sense of self-sufficiency.

Although Katie, as was true for the other nuns, would not have been assigned work in the field, she would have had many opportunities to observe the extensive farm operations, including animal husbandry, planting and harvesting, and the expectations of hired hands—schooling her for her own future endeavors.[26] She would have developed skills in time management and housekeeping chores. Dirty clothes and pots and dishware were simply not left lying around. Floors were swept clean, and gardens carefully tended. Martin knew well that a wife snatched from the convent had a head start on ordinary town or country girls. The highly regimented life of the convent was in many ways superb training for young women. And although it was no life of ease, it certainly did not carry with it the long days of drudgery a girl in poor circumstances would have endured at home. For them, there would have been no books, no Latin instruction, no group singing, no time to set aside for the luxury of prayer and meditation.[27]

On the surface, Katie's lifestyle suffered with marriage. She may have worked long days in the Cranach household, but the home was very comfortable and the meals no doubt tasty and nourishing. How different things were in her new home. The Augustinian monastery was in disrepair, and what furnishings remained were worn and virtually worthless. When they left, the monks had divvied up furnishings and hauled them away. One particular item had apparently not tempted them: "The straw in Luther's bed had not been aired . . . for a year, so that it was rotting from the moisture of his sweat."[28] From the luxurious Cranach mansion to this! But Katie surely must have known what she was getting into, and now she was the one in charge. She reportedly commented, "I must train the Doctor differently, so that he does what I want."[29] She was accused of being demanding, and apparently one of the first of her demands was to order new linen and a mattress from a supplier out of town.[30]

What she probably had not realized before they were married was how entirely inept her new husband was in financial matters. Within months, his resources were so low that they could barely make ends meet. And in the midst of such poverty, he co-signed loans for friends and ended up owing (due to their defaulting) a significant amount of money. He pawned some of their wedding presents, but even then, the debt was only half paid. Part of the problem was that in his transformation from monk to preacher, his remuneration for pulpit ministry remained the same—nothing at all. Finally in 1528, perhaps at Katie's urging, he preached a sermon characterizing himself "as a beggar and threatened to abandon the pulpit."[31]

So dismal were the Luther finances that Martin at one point decided he would moonlight as a woodworker. He ordered a quality lathe from Nuremberg, despite the fact that they desperately needed every extra gulden for household expenses. When the device was delivered to his workshop some time later, he realized that it required skills he did not possess. Indeed, Luther as a craftsman would never become part of Reformation lore.[32]

Finances wasn't the only concern of the Luthers in the mid-1520s. The Reformation itself had seen many setbacks. "Gone were the apparently limitless horizons of the first years, the endless astonishing triumphs in adversity," writes Andrew Pettegree. "The years of adversity of the mid-1520s had changed all that: the limitations of Luther's movement . . . had been cruelly exposed. Luther's enemies in the old church were now irreconcilable and had been joined by an increasing number whose hopes of sharing the new evangelical freedoms had been cruelly dashed."[33]

But it was during these difficult years of theological setbacks and financial difficulties that their family life began to settle down, with its own set of setbacks. Indeed, before they had celebrated their fourth anniversary, Katie had given birth three times and had grievously mourned the death of her second infant, Elizabeth, at eight months. The year was 1528, the same year a scurrilous tract was widely circulated and she also received a personal letter from a well-known Catholic cleric. "The words [were] written August 10, 1528 by Joachim von der Heyden to Catherine Bora, to the effect that she had betaken herself to Wittenberg like a dancing girl and had lived with Luther in open and flagrant immorality before taking him as her husband."[34] The writer went on to report that "the Bora woman," who had apparently learned of "his wiving" other women "is described as bitterly lip braiding him for his faithlessness and dragging him away with her."[35] Amid her poverty and sorrow, Katie could not get away from the vicious, wagging tongues in Wittenberg and far beyond.

And the negative press continued long after her death and by individuals who should have known better than to dismiss her as though her role in the marriage was negligible.

Søren Kierkegaard, for one, had suggested Katharina was of no real account—that "Luther might just as well have married a plank."[36] That Luther was not in love with her at the time of his marriage is common knowledge, and that he married, in part, to demonstrate his support of clerical marriage is certainly true. But to make such a reference regarding Katie is absurd. A nineteenth-century philosopher, Kierkegaard has been accused by some of being a misogynist. Whether true or not, he seriously misjudged the monumental influence Katie had on Martin.

It is tempting to imagine what the Luther marriage might have been like if Martin had attempted to put his doctrine of male headship into practice. Might it have played out in Shakespearian terms? As the story goes, the married Katherina is very different from the sassy single woman she had once been. Then she was an independent, assertive, feisty woman of noble birth who turned into a submissive, compliant bride, though only after her calculating and conniving husband employed his psychological schemes to tame her. If the great Reformer ever imagined his wife to be a shrew, he was surely conscious of his inability to tame her, as Shakespeare's pen tamed his Katherina in *The Taming of the Shrew*.

In actual practice, Luther's view of marriage was one of mutuality. He never appears to have even attempted to tame his wife, though he certainly recognized personality and psychological differences. He liked to poke fun at the trials of marriage, and he imagined it all began with Adam and Eve, who bickered for some nine hundred years over whose fault it was to eat the fruit.[37] For Adam and Eve, there was apparent equality in squabbling. So also with Martin and Katie.

Wives historically (and today) have been deemed of lesser value than husbands. We might imagine that the path toward equality has steadily moved forward. But it could be argued that women enjoyed more equality in sixteenth-century Reformation Germany than they did among their religious successors, whether Puritans or Victorians. Unlike many Victorian women, who were identified only as *Mrs.* So-and-So (exasperating the historian), Katharina von Bora and sixteenth-century women generally were known by their own names. Many were known for having an attitude. Their bossiness or contrariness was often regarded more amusing or annoying than sinful (as with Puritans) or indecent (as with Victorians). Generalizations, true. But the path forward for women's equality was not one paved with steady progress.

There is no doubt that Katie has been given short shrift alongside Martin, though not necessarily so much during their twenty-year marriage. Indeed, she was respected and regarded by many, for good or ill, as the go-to individual for important business and household matters. Widowhood, however, seriously diminished her status. And in the generations since, she has very often been overlooked. Yet her marriage to Luther profoundly changed the slant of Reformed belief and practice. How would Luther be remembered today had he remained a single man, had he not taken that monumental decision to marry Katharina von Bora? And one wonders if any other woman could have served as such a competent partner in both his marriage and ministry.

Today, in an era of good feelings among Catholics and Protestants, we like to emphasize what we have in common. But Roman Catholicism is and was wrong regarding married clergy. The implication that true holiness requires celibacy has led to serious sexual abuse within the priesthood. Sure, Protestants have had their own sex scandals, but it has not been fostered by a false requirement for celibate clergy.

The marriage of Martin and Katie turned out to be anything but a scandal, as their enemies claimed it was. Indeed, more than any other act, save posting of the ninety-five theses, their marriage defined the Reformation. Katie's role cannot be overstated. Truly theirs is the premier marriage of the Reformation. "This is perhaps most visibly evident," writes Elizabeth Plummer, "in the multiple double portraits of Martin Luther and Katharina von Bora produced between 1525 and 1529, showing the pair as a typical married couple of [their] social status."[38]

A typical sixteenth-century married couple? Hardly. And Katharina, a typical Protestant wife? Not at all. She was too confident and independent. She went about her life simply assuming she was the equal of her husband, and any man for that matter. Word on the street was that she was bossy, domineering, given to henpecking her husband. She wore the trousers, they said, and made the final family decisions. They might have even called her a daughter of Eve or a Jezebel. For sure, they did not describe her as a sweet, subdued, submissive lady—the docile and weak wife of the great Reformer. And here I challenge Laurel Thatcher Ulrich's oft-quoted line: "Well-behaved women seldom make history."[39]

Had Katie, as we shall later see, been "well-behaved," she would indeed have made history and would have been more frequently referenced by her husband's colleagues and others who knew her. If she were an ideal Christian wife of the great Reformer, biographers would not be struggling to find sources. As we have discovered, however, she was virtually written out of history by her contemporaries.

CHAPTER

"Neither Wood nor Stone"

A REFORMATION HUSBAND

By the grace of God," Martin Luther wrote in his commentary on Genesis 2:22, "everyone declares that it is something good and holy to live with one's wife in harmony and peace."[1] Luther, with all his flaws and bombast, modeled how to live with a wife in such harmony and peace. Indeed, he made a concerted effort to do just that, all the while often driving Katie to distraction. "God put fingers on our hands," he once remarked, "for the money to slide through them so God can give us more."[2] Then again, he commented to a friend, "I have patched this pair of pants four times myself. I will patch them again before I have new ones made."[3] He was both careless with money and frugal at the same time. As to the patching, Katie was furious because the material was cut from their son's trousers. In many respects, Luther seemed to be clueless as a husband. Yet if we compare him to other husbands of his day, we know Katie could have done much worse.

Had I been a sixteenth-century nun transported in a wagon to Wittenberg, would I have set my sights on marrying Martin Luther? I have actually contemplated that question. Some might consider him a real catch—the greatest religious thinker since Saint Paul, Saint Augustine, and Saint Thomas Aquinas. He was a man who more than any other sought to walk amid great opposition in the footsteps of Paul. But husband material? I doubt it. Nor would I have set my sights on marrying Paul himself had I been one of his admirers in the

90

first century. Such a prospect would never have occurred to me, had I not become familiar with the writings of the renowned Henrietta Mears—the founder of Gospel Light Publishing and a highly esteemed Bible teacher and mentor to hundreds of young men, including Billy Graham and Bill Bright. When one of her "boys" kidded her about not being married, she quipped that she had never found anyone who could hold a candle to the apostle Paul.[4]

Like Luther, Paul had issues, at least if we are to take seriously his confession in Romans: "I am unspiritual, sold as a slave to sin. I do not understand what I do. For what I want to do I do not do, but what I hate I do . . . For I do not do the good I want to do, but the evil I do not want to do—this I keep on doing . . . What a wretched man I am!" (7:14–15, 19, 24). What his sins were we are left to wonder. In Luther's case, he sinned *boldly*, as he at one point directed another to do: "Be a sinner and sin boldly but believe and rejoice in Christ even more boldly."[5] Even Paul would have been shocked, particularly if he had taken at face value the words of the devout Catholic Sir Thomas More. James Reston Jr. offers this colorful summary:

> In a tract of more than three hundred pages called *Responsio ad Lutherum*, published in 1523, [More] called Luther "a pig, a dolt, and a liar," an "ape," "drunkard," "a pestilential buffoon," and "lousy little friar." Luther's writings, wrote the judicious Sir Thomas, came from snippets he gleaned in brothels, barber shops, taverns, and privies. In his notebooks the monk wrote down anything he heard when a coachman spoke "ribaldly," or a servant "insolently," or "a whore wantonly," or a pimp "indecently," or a bath-keeper "filthily," or a shitter "obscenely." And then, as if he had not got his point across sufficiently, More lost his literary and lawyerly composure entirely when he wrote, "For as long as your reverend paternity is determined to tell these shameless lies, others are permitted on behalf of his English majesty, to throw back into your paternity's shitty mouth, truly the shit-pool of

all shit, all the muck and shit which your damnable rottenness has vomited up."[6]

More's contempt and Luther's crude behavior aside, the Reformer truly was in many respects a great man. But it does not follow that great men necessarily make great husbands. The Luthers, however, seem to have had one of those singular marriages we speak of as having been made in heaven.

Truly, he did have his good points as a husband, particularly for one who had not yet emerged from medieval boorishness (and we give him some slack on that account). He quickly recognized Katie's capabilities and sometimes expressed virtual adoration for her. This is perhaps most clearly seen in his profound regard for Paul's letter to the Galatians, referring to it as "my Katherine von Bora."[7] Again he confessed, "I give more credit to Katherine than to Christ, who has done so much more for me."[8]

Likewise, Luther promoted romance. More than that, he sponsored and marketed it. In the early 1520s, when confined in Wartburg Castle, Luther wrote to one of his supporters, Nicolas Gerbel:

> Kiss and rekiss your wife . . . Let her love and be loved. You are fortunate in having overcome, by an honorable marriage, that celibacy in which one is a prey to devouring fires and to unclean ideas. That unhappy state of a single person, male or female, reveals to me each hour of the day so many horrors, that nothing sounds in my ear as bad as the name of monk or nun or priest. A married life is a paradise, even where all else is wanting.[9]

There was no biblical precedent for "that celibacy," but there was for kissing and rekissing one's wife. Doesn't the Bible tell us that Isaac fondled Rebekah? (Genesis 26:8), Luther once asked. In fact, Luther sounded downright risqué: "We are permitted to laugh and have fun with and embrace our wives, whether they are naked or clothed," and if you are depressed and "can find help for yourself by thinking of a girl, do so."[10]

That Luther would be so transformed from a monk into an affectionate husband is nothing short of amazing. Everything he learned from his earliest childhood in the Catholic faith had focused on sexual gratification as a sin. "When I was a boy," he wrote, "the wicked and impure practice of celibacy had made marriage so disreputable that I believed that I could not even think about the life of married people without sinning. Everybody was fully persuaded that anyone who intended to lead a holy life acceptable to God could not get married."[11]

But too much passion, he knew, was not always a good thing: "I have observed many married couples coming together in such great passion that they were ready to devour each other for love, but after a half year the one ran away from the other." Some couples lasted longer—ones "who have become hostile to each other after they had five or six children and were bound to each other not merely by marriage but also by the fruits of their union. Yet they left each other."[12] Marriage was little different then than it is today. But for the Luthers, marriage was a source of deep and abiding love, until death did them part.

One reason Martin can be viewed as a model husband to Katie is that he served her. We read time and again of his bowing to her desires, and he held in high regard a humble way of life. In fact, an important aspect of Luther's theological underpinnings was his emphasis on the sacred in everyday life. William Lazareth notes that whether working in the fields or over a hot oven, these were the ordinary and humble duties that served as a backdrop in the life of Jesus.[13] Luther's daily life illustrates his theology: "Luther's faith was simple enough to trust that after a conscientious day's labor, a Christian father could come home and eat his sausage, drink his beer, play his flute, sing with his children, and make love to his wife—all to the glory of God!"[14]

Here Luther is represented as a typical German husband and father who comes home to supper after a day's work. But Luther also frequently represented a typical German hausfrau. Any mother today could wish that her husband had such a modern perspective on fatherhood as Luther did—and not simply to relieve an overworked wife, but because it was embedded in his very theology:

> Now observe that when that clever harlot, our natural reason, . . . takes a look at married life, she turns up her nose and says, "Alas, must I rock the baby, wash its diapers, make its bed, smell its stench, stay up nights with it, take care of it when it cries, heal its rashes and sores, and on top of that care for my wife, provide for her . . . What, should I make such a prisoner of myself? O you poor, wretched fellow . . .
>
> What then does Christian Faith say to this? . . . It says, O God . . . I confess to thee that I am not worthy to rock the little babe or wash its diapers, or to be entrusted with the care of the child and its mother . . . O how gladly will I do so, though the duties should be even more insignificant and despised.[15]

These words are astounding for the sixteenth century, and from a former monk. Marriage was a partnership pure and simple—God's will. No Christian man should ever imagine that the wife alone is responsible for the "insignificant and despised" duties of changing diapers and staying up nights. Pretending to speak for a dutiful Catholic, Luther declaimed sarcastically, "Fie, fie upon such wretchedness and bitterness! It is better to remain free and lead a peaceful, carefree life; I will become a priest or a nun and compel my children to do likewise."[16] Yes, children. The line is dripping with sarcasm.

Luther not only shared with Katie household tasks and child care, but he also went out of his way to offer little gestures of thoughtfulness, she in return doing the same for him. On one occasion, when she had expressed her hankering for oranges, he ordered them from Nuremberg, knowing they were unavailable in Wittenberg. And why not? "Why should he not be glad to do her bidding, for was she not dearer to him than the King of France or Venice?"[17]

Even before he laid eyes on Katie, however, Luther honored family values. It was difficult to disobey his earthly father to follow what he perceived to be the call of his heavenly Father—a call to become a monk. But while frantically pursuing this vocation, he did not diminish family values. In his late twenties, when he visited Rome, his parents were on his mind. Later he claimed he spent hours saying Masses for his parents, almost wishing them dead so he could have saved them from purgatory. He would have been particularly blessed, as it was widely believed, if he had read a Saturday Mass at St. John's. The lines, however, were too long. So, as he later recalled, "I ate a smoked herring instead."[18]

One might be tempted to think Luther penned this somewhat tongue-in-cheek reflection to emphasize what a completely devoted monk he was. By the time he had written it, he had certainly developed a low view of the moral cesspool he found at Rome, and all its hourly rituals and relics too many to count. His last line—"so I ate smoked herring"—is almost a dead giveaway. If he had really thought he could make his mother *blessed*, he would have waited, no matter how long the line.

Truly, Luther did love his parents and could be said to have revered his father. But his mother was duly acknowledged, even though he did not so easily forget how harsh her discipline was when he was a child. His final letter to his mother during her last illness is touching, and the reference to Katie and the children speaks for itself. After giving his mother a lengthy blessing, asking God to grant her strong faith, he adds, "All my children and my Katy pray for you. Some cry, some eat and say, grandmother is very sick."[19]

In June 1530, when Martin was away, Katie received a letter from her husband's traveling companion. It brought the sad news that Martin's father had died. After Martin received the news, his friend reported that "he said to me, 'My father is dead.' And then he took his Psalter and went to his room and wept so much that for two days he couldn't work."[20]

Luther's big heart was certainly not limited to his love of family. He was generous with friends and strangers alike and was particularly concerned for those on the lower rungs of society. This is evident in his translation work and catechism. Unlike medieval scholars who wrote for other scholars, Luther focused extensively on the unschooled, as is manifest in his *Small Catechism*. When traveling and visiting local parishes, he was astonished by biblical and doctrinal ignorance. "What manifold misery I beheld! The common people, especially in the villages, have no knowledge whatever of Christian doctrine, and, alas! many pastors are altogether incapable and incompetent to teach."[21]

His concern also extended to the physical needs of the poor. When a lawyer friend helped procure justice for a poor woman, Luther wrote to thank him, assuring him that he would one day receive a rich reward for not only responding favorably to his appeal but also for sending him a cask of his own brewed beer. Such a fine gift, Luther adds, may have been more appropriately given to the poor. Undeserving as he is, however, he will have no problem finding a good use for it.[22]

Luther's kindness was also seen in his letters that often included pastoral counsel. To friends and acquaintances he wrote in a very personal style, confessing his own struggles and offering words of compassion and consolation. On one occasion, having been in contact with a former nun, Elizabeth von Canitz, whom he hoped would organize a school for girls, he wrote, "I hear too that the evil one is assailing you with melancholy. O my dear woman, do not let him terrify you, for whoever suffers from the devil here will not suffer from him yonder. It is a good sign."[23]

He was not ashamed to admit that sometimes the counselor was the one most in need of counseling, and that very fact reveals much about Luther as husband. On one occasion, with students at the table, he confessed, "I, Doctor Luther, have been in such high temptations and *Anfechtungen* that they consumed my whole body so that I could hardly breathe, and no one could console me." Was he the only one, he wondered, who experienced such sadness?[24]

Katie was a competent village healer, and not surprisingly her most difficult patient was her husband. In addition to his black moods and cavernous bouts of doubt (*Anfechtungen*), he was throughout most of their married life weakened by one malady after another—maladies exacerbated by overeating and circulatory issues.[25] Depression and spiritual despair, however, were not new to the married Luther. How much Katie knew of his past problems is unknown, but while he was at the Wartburg Castle (when Katie was still at the Marienthron convent), he suffered spiritually, psychologically, and physically. To Melanchthon he had written:

> I see myself insensible, hardened, sunk in idleness, alas! seldom in prayer, and not venting one groan over God's Church. My unsubdued flesh burns me with devouring fire. In short, I . . . am devoured by the flesh, by luxury, indolence, idleness, somnolence. Is it that God has turned away from me, because you no longer pray for me? You must take my place; you, richer in God's gifts, and more acceptable in his sight. Here, a week has passed away since I put pen to paper, since I have prayed or studied, either vexed by fleshly cares, or by other temptations.[26]

At the Wartburg Castle and throughout his life, Luther's depressive moods were exacerbated by his strong belief in a very real personal devil. That he may have thrown an ink pot at the devil doesn't begin to capture his struggle with a subversive and seditious underworld of spirit darkness. He almost seemed to revel in repeating accounts that could be summed up in "Acts of the Devil." This ever-present evil personage once consumed more than half a wagon load of a poor peasant's hay, and for apparently no good reason, he soured milk and butter.[27]

Some of these "Acts" were drawn from his memories from childhood. In one instance, a pregnant woman had given birth to a dormouse because the family had captured one of these nocturnal rodents and tied a bell around its neck to scare off others of its kind. When the bell-ringing rodent suddenly appeared and scared the woman, her unborn baby was magically transformed into the very critter she wanted to be rid of. Such claims were assumed to be true and often added to the very real fears of pregnant women.[28]

One wonders if the very pragmatic, down-to-earth Katie rolled her eyes at such stories. We do learn, however, that her husband called on her on occasion to help eradicate the devil. "Try as hard as you can to despise these thoughts sent by Satan," he wrote in 1530 to Jerome Weller, living nearby in Wittenberg. "By all means flee solitude, for he lies in wait most for those alone. This devil is conquered by despising and mocking him, not by resisting and arguing." His next words are somewhat bewildering: "Therefore, Jerome, joke and play games with my wife and others, in which way you will drive out your diabolic thoughts and take courage."[29]

What does this say about the overwhelmed Katie with household tasks and little ones underfoot? It sounds as though she would be prepared at a moment's notice to laugh and play games with a seriously depressed neighbor (who had once boarded with her). But Martin had other pointers as well: "drink more, or joke and talk nonsense, or do some other merry things. Sometimes we must drink more, sport, recreate ourselves, aye, and even sin a little to spite the devil."[30] He was truly convinced that a stein of Wittenberg beer would do wonders and so also could contemplation on pretty girls or singing some hearty (and most likely ribald) bar tunes. As a last resort, do listen to a preacher known for humor and wit.

Dormouse babies and sour milk notwithstanding, Luther was capable of having a more rational train of mind. Unlike Philip Melanchthon, he took no stock in astrology.[31] Though easily swayed by superstitions and preposterous claims that were rumored about, Luther conceded that he had often been taken for a fool and was not proud of that fact.[32]

There is an oft-told story about Katie and her ability to calm her husband during dark moods. My favorite version is found in an 1884 edition of *The Sabbath School Magazine*, edited by William Keddie:

> Luther at one time was sorely vexed by the wickedness of the world, and by the dangers that beset the Church. One morning, he saw his wife dressed in mourning. Surprised, he asked her who had died. "Do you not know?" she replied. "God in heaven is dead." "How can you talk such nonsense, Katie?" Luther replied; "How can God die? He is immortal, and will live through all eternity." "Is that really true?" she asked.—"Of course," he said, still not perceiving what she was aiming at; "how can you doubt it? As surely as there is a God in heaven, so sure it is that He can never die." "And yet," she said, "though you do not doubt that, you are hopeless and discouraged." His wife's little stratagem had the desired effect of restoring his confidence and trust in God.[33]

Although this magazine was "designed for the use of teachers, adult scholars, and parents," children no doubt heard the same story about Katie, one passed down into the twenty-first century. And it's the same story my sister-in-law immediately remembered on hearing I was writing this book: "Oh, have you heard the story about Katie dressed in mourning?"

Luther's physical ailments, as well as his depression, were serious, and their recurrences scared the daylights out of Katie. In the late autumn of 1528, he was seriously handicapped by a disorder known today as Ménière's disease, an inner-ear ailment that manifests itself in vertigo and tinnitus (dizziness and ringing in the ears). He also had problems with ulcers, indigestion, constipation, and other maladies, especially as a younger man. The last ten years of his life, he suffered from kidney stones, gout, arthritis, hemorrhoids, and heart problems, and if that weren't enough to lay him low, he was beset with catarrh, an inflammation of the nose and throat. Katie sought to treat him with whatever remedies she learned might help, and she worried.

In addition to caring for his physical and emotional needs, Katie provided a very stable home. Her good humor and hospitality did wonders for him, as did children and routine family life. They enjoyed the ordinary amusements of youth: card games, chess, outdoor ball games, dancing, and playacting. He approved of activities that involved interaction between boys and girls, ones that would prepare them for adult life. Dating, however was severely restricted. A partner, he strongly believed, must be approved by the parents—no secretive courtship and marriage. Reading was another activity he heartily supported. Stories like Aesop's fables were entertaining, as well as morally uplifting.

Another aspect of family life involved pets, especially their beloved dog Tölpel, often mentioned in Luther's *Table Talk*. As an object lesson, Martin once contrasted his dog's gulping down table scraps with his own apathy in prayer. The story is also told of how a child once asked whether her dog would go to heaven. He reached down and commented as he petted the dog, "Be quiet, bundchen, and at the resurrection you, too, shall have a golden tail."[34]

As a father, Luther admitted his own motherliness at times, and in the following letter, we see this fatherly feminine side of him. While away from home for some months at Coburg, he wrote to young Hans. He was not admonishing him to behave as he sometimes had done. Rather, he communicated with the six-year-old boy through a delightful story:

> Grace and peace in Christ, my dear little son. I hear with great pleasure that you are learning your lessons so well, and praying so diligently. Continue to do so, my son, and cease not. When I come home I will bring you a nice present from the fair. I know a beautiful garden, where there are a great many children in fine little coats, and they go under the trees and gather beautiful apples and pears, cherries and plums; they sing and run about

and are as happy as they can be. Sometimes they ride on nice little ponies, with golden bridles and silver saddles. I asked the man whose garden it is: "What little children are these?" And he told me, "They are little children who love to pray and learn and are good." When I said, "My dear sir, I have a little boy at home; his name is little Hans Luther; would you let him come into the garden, too, to eat some of these nice apples and pears, and ride on these fine little ponies, and play with these children?" The man said, "If he loves to say his prayers and learn his lessons, and is a good boy, he may come."[35]

Family was central to Luther's reforms. Other reformers had come and gone, but none so emphasized the matter of marriage and family. Indeed, no previous reformer had raised the issue of family as the focal point of creation and Scripture. He stood as the giant of family values.

Clearly Katie stands alongside him in this regard—adding flesh and blood to theology. Without her, Martin's teaching on marriage and family would have been little more than a skeleton. And no other woman could have so profoundly molded his mind and his daily habits. This is a critical point. His words mimicked medieval tradition. The husband reigns over wife and family. But for Katie and Martin, mutuality sparkled in every aspect of daily life. Of course, he occasionally reminded his friends and her that he was the head, maybe even the man of the house. Sure. She had no problem with that—as long as he didn't interfere with her agenda.

When we seek to sum up Martin Luther as husband and family man, his actions speak louder than his words. His words are those of male headship and female submission. From his letters and the remarks of others, Luther was remarkably dependent on Katie. He confided in her and trusted her judgment like that of no one else. He was very frequently, in the minds of many of his friends, too submissive to her. Addressing her as Herr Käthe, he "wittingly exchanged the masculine role for the feminine."[36]

Luther had a more open attitude toward sex than did his Catholic counterparts. But that did not mean that anything goes. He did have certain standards, though it is not that he followed such rules in his own marriage: "They should not disrobe for sex, they should not try to arouse one another unduly, they should not turn the marriage bed into 'a manure heap and a sow bath' by resorting to unusual techniques and positions."[37]

Elsewhere in his advice column, he was more easygoing about intimate activities between husband and wife. When attacks of despair seized him, he sometimes "embraced his wife naked in bed," writes Richard Marius, "and these depressions sent from the devil fled away." He was convinced that his ability to prevail over Satan was greatly aided by being in bed with Katie.[38]

Apart from his wedding night when Justus Jonas and perhaps others witnessed Martin and Katie consummate their marriage, Martin was typically tight-lipped about his sex life with his wife. He did, however, write a very private letter to her when he was ill, less than two weeks before he died. The matter was his impotence, and he suggested she confide in Philip Melanchthon, who could advise her, having apparently discussed this very private matter with his close friend before. Reading between the lines of Luther's letters, it can be inferred that sexual intimacies were an important aspect of their marriage until nearly the end.[39]

Martin and Katie are an interesting study in opposites, but one of the most unusual differences relates to friendships. Compared to her husband, Katie had very few friends. Biographers have sought to argue otherwise, though the case is weak. But there is no doubt that her husband had very close friends, and not the male buddies of today who get together only to watch football, play golf, or shoot some hoops. He had intimate friends with whom he corresponded and held in close confidence.

He also had drinking pals, though apparently he never caroused about town with them. Indeed, it was at the Black Cloister where he found Katie's beer the best-brewed in town. He liked to impress fellow drinkers that he could hold his beer. He liked to fill his stein of beer for the glory of God, toasting the Lord's Prayer if it were full up, the Apostles' Creed if he did not fill it so full—and if prudence prevailed, he filled it only to the Ten Commandments marker.[40] He apparently could get all the way to the Lord's Prayer without falling down.

So how do we sum up Martin Luther? To those at table one evening, he offered a short autobiographical summary that indicates the twists and turns of his life—a life that not even astrologers could have predicted. He chose to emphasize his humble background, describing his father, grandfather, and great-grandfather all as peasants. He told of how his father wanted him to become a lawyer. But much to his father's chagrin, he became a monk, "and then [he] got into the pope's hair and married an apostate nun. Who could have read that in the stars?"[41]

As a husband and father, Luther put his Reformation teaching into practice. His focus on the family in his home and in his biblical theology has stood the test of time. But there was no Martin Luther Jr. who stood out among his sons or descendants—no son to ignite another Reformation. No namesake to carry on—that is, not until another boy was renamed Martin Luther Jr. In 1934, when Baptist preacher Michael King was visiting Europe, he was profoundly stirred by the story of Martin Luther—indeed, so stirred that he changed his name from Michael to Martin Luther and at the same time changed his son's name to Martin Luther King Jr.

This five-year-old boy would one day become a preacher himself and bring about another reformation that, like the first, continues to reverberate through religious and civil life. His philosophy mirrors Luther's own: "There are some things so dear, some things so precious, some things so eternally true, that they are worth dying for. And I submit to you that if a man has not discovered something that he will die for, he isn't fit to live."[42]

CHAPTER 7

"From Katie, a Little Heathen"

MOTHERHOOD AT THE MANSE

My baby. *Mine* . . . There was a fierceness to the love that was born the instant I saw him," writes Sue Hubbell. "It was uncivilized, crude, unquestioning, unreasoning. I first began to understand it when . . . we were on a family camping trip, and during the night were awakened by an old sow bear . . . Her baby had strayed on the other side of our tent. She was frantic, fierce, angry, and . . . dangerous." Hubbell speaks of her own maternal instincts and then comments, "I had to learn to keep the old sow bear under control."[1] Sow-bear mothers are not necessarily the most lovable. They may not be known for baking cupcakes and singing sweet lullabies. My mother was in some ways a sow bear, myself also. So was Katie. She was protective and stern.

Growing up on a farm as one of five children, I resonate in many ways with the Luther children. My mother had a strong personality and ruled the family, sometimes with an iron fist. She worked in the fields and gardens while managing the house full of kids. She canned fruits and vegetables, butchered chickens, sewed and mended clothes and curtains, all the while being active in the community and, while not being particularly religious, attending church every week. She was a strict mother whose unqualified devotion to her children often seemed to be all that mattered.

Katharina von Bora brought those same qualities to motherhood, the most essential facet of her life. We easily focus on her role as wife of the great Reformer because he has been such a central figure in Christianity, and truly she did fill a prominent place in that realm. But her own focus was primarily on her children from the time of her pregnancy in 1525 to her death in 1553. One of the reasons her role as mother is overlooked is that none of her children became famous—especially famous sons. From biblical times into the twentieth century, the test of motherhood has rested on that achievement.

Katie pales in comparison to Susanna Wesley, the ultimate Christian mother. Indeed, Susanna was the mother of all reality shows—an eighteenth-century version of nineteen kids and counting. Katie had only six children, although when we count all the orphans and others under her roof, she was not far behind Susanna. There are other significant similarities, however. Both women were married to ministers and presided over a manse with farm and acreage that doubled as a home school. Both were proficient in gardening, herbal remedies, and animal husbandry. Both were accused of being prideful and both talked back to their husbands.

Katie, however, was not a stay-at-home mother. She was often absent for days or weeks at a time to handle business at her properties, sometimes leaving Martin in charge of the children. Susanna stayed put while her husband left home, accused by some of being little more than a ne'er-do-well. Susanna preached on occasion when her husband was away, something Katie never would have done. And unlike Susanna, Katie didn't write her rules of child rearing, nor did she write letters that are today available to our prying eyes.

But the most important difference was that Susanna, unlike Katie, was the mother of two famous sons, John and Charles Wesley. John spoke of his mother as a "preacher of righteousness" who had a profound influence on his ministry.

If we could bring Katie and Susanna together, I think they would find they have much in common and a lot to talk about. Would Susanna confide to Katie that, with all her fame as a superwoman, her husband abandoned her for a time and her children one after another had serious problems in adulthood, including mental instability and broken marriages—even son John himself? Would Katie share her own difficulties with children and her fears for her husband's physical and mental well-being?

Despite the 170 years that separated their birth dates (1499–1669), living conditions had not changed significantly. This is a major point to ponder as we consider Katie and other historical figures. If we jump to 170 years after Susanna's birth, we arrive at 1839, where we would find ten-year-old Catherine Mumford, who would grow up to marry William Booth. She would also have a slew of children—and would also talk back to her husband. Here again we would discover lower- and middle-class women still living not so differently from Katie and Susanna, toiling from dawn to dark with few modern conveniences. In fact, the Industrial Revolution was driving families to the cities, and the standard of living often took a serious dive.

But jump ahead (in Germany, England—or North America) another 170 years to 2009, and we see a dizzying display of progress for mothers and daughters. Education, transportation, communication, medical breakthroughs, cheap manufactured goods—all of these things tangled up in the crazy concept of gender equality. For a woman today, sitting down with Katie, Susanna, and Catherine would be looking from the outside in. They would resonate with each other, while we would be seen as aliens from a distant future.

Yet women today, myself included, want to claim Katie as our own. "Sisters of Katie Luther," a website with several contributors, views Katie as one who would today support traditional gender roles. In a post titled "Why I Am Not a Pastor," Katy Schumpert writes:

> I hope that when you read the title of this piece, you said to
> yourself, "Well, of course she's not a pastor—she's a woman!" But
> in these (shades of) gray and latter days, when we have discarded
> all the "traditional gender roles" God has ordained and which

have served us for so many millennia, not only do fewer and fewer people react that way, but more and more people get downright apoplectic that anyone would have such a reaction. I used to be one of them.[2]

From Katie, the "sisters" draw support for homeschooling and being stay-at-home mothers, though she herself was hardly "traditional" in that regard. We do clearly see her hovering over sickly children, her husband, and other members of the large extended family. But these are natural responses in routine family life. She was by nature fierce and protective of her children. What we don't see is motherhood drawn from traditional gender roles—a motherhood "God has ordained," ruled by a theological or biblical perspective.

With most mothers, there is a primal love that comes naturally with the birth of a child. Martin Luther, observing Katie, likened this to God's love for the sinner—God, who sees beyond our sins, even as a mother loves her child in spite of grunge and dirty diapers.[3]

We cannot assess Katie as mother apart from Martin as father. Unlike the circumstances relating to Susanna Wesley, there is scant record of Katie's child-rearing philosophy or practice. She is full of deeds as a parent, as Martin is, but he is also full of words. He reportedly said on one occasion, "Child what have you done that I should love you so? What with your befowling the corners and bawling through the whole house?"[4] In 1538, he commented, "Christ said we must become as little children to enter the kingdom of heaven. Dear God, have we got to become such idiots?"[5]

For Katie, such humorous remarks from her husband were commonplace, and there is no evidence that she would have disagreed with him. But for her, there was work to do. His reputation was largely based on his words; hers was based on her work. She was always at work, and child care was accomplished amid other tasks and always, by today's standards, under primitive circumstances. It was a time when medical care and matters of hygiene had not advanced beyond medieval customs. Childbirth was a perilous endeavor, and babies and mothers who survived were considered fortunate indeed. Katie, a healthy bride in her mid-twenties, was an exception. Except for one instance, childbirth for her was essentially routine—routine, that is, for the sixteenth century.

The record shows that she gave birth to six children in the years 1526, 1527, 1529, 1531, 1533, and 1534 (three sons and three daughters, though only one daughter would survive beyond her teen years). Although certainly not a record of rapid births, we can imagine Katie had her hands full. A natural form of birth control was assumed to be breastfeeding. She was still nursing little Martin, however, when she became pregnant with Paul. At the end of her childbearing came the most difficult of all her pregnancies—one resulting in a miscarriage. Miscarriages in the early months are often not even recognized, so we assume she was well along in her pregnancy. So severe were the complications that she nearly died, a situation that allowed the couple no time to mourn or to hardly acknowledge the little one they had lost.[6]

But life did not wait for her while she was recovering. For a time, she crawled on the floor to go from room to room, making sure the children were cared for. Only after several months was she finally fully restored to good health. The fact that she was past forty at the time and beyond normal childbearing age likely contributed to the miscarriage and her slow recovery.

Although wealthy women often employed wet nurses, breastfeeding was the custom of the day. For Martin, however, the matter was more than a cultural norm. It was a God-ordained expectation: "It is therefore unkind and unnatural for a mother not to nurse her child, for God gave her her breasts and her milk for that purpose; unless she is unable to do it."[7] Apart from breastfeeding, there were servants who helped out and, above all others, "Auntie Lena" von Bora. The little ones apparently clung to her with great affection so that their father became almost jealous of her.

Katie and Martin had wasted no time in getting their family

started. Hans was born in June 1526, less than a year after they married. In a letter to a friend, he announced the blessed news. It might have been a time for him to wax eloquent, except for the fact that he had to cut the letter short because the ailing Katie was calling for him to come to her aid.[8]

As soon as she was notified, Martin's mother traveled from Mansfield to help out her new daughter-in-law. The birth had gone well, not so nursing the infant. Like so many new mothers, she simply did not have enough milk. Martin lamented the fact, saying God should charge for all the good things he gives people—a wife, a child, eye, foot, hand, etc.: "I'd pay [God] 100 florin if he'd give Katie more milk."[9]

Martin placed no blame on her, but rather praised her for motherly capabilities, observing that a mother could obviously manage child care better with one finger than a father with clenched fists.[10] Martin was a doting father, often making mention of his firstborn son in correspondence. He was proud as a peacock when he announced, "Hans is cutting his teeth and beginning to make a joyous nuisance of himself. These are the joys of marriage of which the pope is not worthy."[11] Later, Katie must have found his antics to be less than joyous. "When little Hans," writes Martin Brecht, "first 'shit' on his own—a facility which he soon tested in every corner—it was worth mentioning in one of his father's letters."[12]

This must have been around the time baby sister Elizabeth was born on December 10, when Hans was eighteen months old. It was a frightful time to give birth—in the midst of a raging plague, but all went well, and Katie quickly bounced back. But deep sorrow came soon enough. The death of baby Elizabeth ten months later was a dark hour at the Black Cloister. There is no record that she was a sickly child. Death apparently came suddenly. Imagine the absolute heartbreak. She's crawling across the floor after big brother Hans. She's standing and taking her first steps, smiling and cackling that baby laugh. And then in August, she's gone. Martin was startled by his own sorrow and deep sentimentality, "almost like a woman."[13] His only comfort was that his daughter was being cared for by God, a perfect father. Whether Katie found such comfort we do not know. How, we wonder, does she move on?

Two months later, however, Katie is pregnant again. On May 4, 1529, daughter Magdalena is born. Here, in 1529, is a point at which we are stopped dead in our tracks. She is thirty years old, three adored little ones, one dead, and what does this year bring? More children and extended family members than any ordinary woman could possibly handle. The Black Cloister was often filled to the brim with relatives and hangers-on, including a half dozen children of Martin's deceased sister. There were also relatives of Katie who were in and out, the most appreciated and permanent being her Aunt Lena, whom Katie had come to know well when they were both nuns at the Nimbschen convent. Of course, students, visiting pastors, professors, and sometimes refugees made up the bulk of the residents who found temporary housing.[14]

Though Katie today is remembered primarily as a wife, her responsibilities as mother to this large brood were truly astounding.

When Luther was residing at Coburg in June 1530, he received mail from home. We know this only from his response to Katie: "I have received Lenchen's picture with the box. At first I could not believe the little lock—it seemed to me so black." At this time, little Magdelena (Lenchen) would have been just over a year old. Her father was away, missing some of her delightful toddler months due to his nearly six-month (from April 23 to October 4) involvement in the Diet of Augsburg. His letter continues: "If you want to stop breast-feeding the baby and wean it, it would be good to do it gradually." On this point he cites Argula von Grumbach, who had recently shared a meal with him.[15] Did Katie really need the advice of a distant noblewoman, having already nursed three babies?

We wonder if, despite his difficult negotiations, she may have begrudged the apparent good time her husband was having in Coburg. She was home during these months, responsible for a full house without him. After he returned, she would soon become pregnant again.

Luther's breezy reflections almost seem to dismiss the costs involved in his rapidly growing immediate and extended family, an outlook that could not have been voiced by Katie: "I am rich. My God has given me a nun and three little children. I don't care that I have a lot of debts, for when my Katya counts them up, another child comes along."[16] Yes indeed. Little Martin, her fourth child, was still breastfeeding in the spring of 1532 when Katie became pregnant with her fifth.

Fortunately, she had household help, servants, and particularly Aunt Lena. But family matters were her responsibility. Although Martin did not regard it beneath him to take charge of household tasks, he referred to Katie's toil and her expertise time and again. She was the one in charge, though they together disciplined the children—discipline with both "rod and apple" side by side.[17] When Katie had time, she joined in games and made music with the children. Indeed, they sang as a small choir. For this very purpose, Luther wrote a well-known Christmas hymn, "From Heaven Above to Earth I Come":

> *To you, this night, is born a child*
> *Of Mary, chosen mother mild;*
> *This little child, of lowly birth,*
> *Shall be the joy of all your earth . . .*
>
> *Ah, dearest Jesus, holy child,*
> *Make thee a bed, soft, undefiled,*
> *Within my heart, that it may be*
> *A quiet chamber kept for thee.*[18]

Speaking for both Katie and himself, he wrote in his "Preface to the German Mass" that discipline and playfulness should go hand in hand. A child psychologist of sorts, he challenged parents to get down on the floor and be one with them.[19]

That Katie revered marriage, family, and home to the degree her husband did can only be inferred. Both emphasized the critical importance of child rearing and good works. Martin repeated the saying that parents could attain eternal life in heaven by doing no more than properly training their children.[20] Caring for children is, in his mind, serving *the least of these*—as it were, the hungry, thirsty, naked, imprisoned, and sick. "O what a blessed marriage and home . . . where such parents were to be found! Truly it would be a real church, a chosen cloister, yea, a paradise."[21] Salvation, paradise, marriage, home.

The most painful sorrow Martin and Katie shared together was the death of Magdalena on September 20, 1542, having celebrated her thirteenth birthday the previous May. If we can trust Lucas Cranach the Elder in his portrait of the girl, she looks like her mother. Although her expression is serious, we can imagine her having inherited her father's quick wit. Yet we know so very little about her, despite all the letters and "table talk" of her famous father. And she seems almost absent in the scenes of sorrow as she nears death. She responds to her father that she is prepared to die and go to heaven, but who was this delightful girl when she was bouncing a little brother in her lap or singing in the family choir as her father played the lute? Who was she when her mother talked to her about her menstrual periods or showed her for the first time how to mend her stockings or bake a batch of strudel?

Apart from the sorrowful death scene, we know very little about this teenage girl from old Wittenberg. Thirteen years earlier, when Luther had asked his friend and pastor Nicolaus von Amsdorf to be her godfather, he endearingly spoke of her as a "little heathen" who needed Nicolaus "to help her [enter] holy Christendom through the heavenly, precious sacrament of baptism."[22]

Here as elsewhere, the biographer of Katharina longs for some insight from her own pen. What were her words—or was she not even able to formulate them—during that time of deep despair when their dear child was dying? As it was, Lenchen breathed her last in her father's arms.

Even in his deepest sorrow, he reportedly prayed and rose above the inevitable loss. If it were God's will, then she should die. Indeed, he told God he would "gladly give her up" to him. And to his daughter he reportedly said, "My dearest child, my own sweet and good 'Lenchen,' I know you would gladly stay with your father here, but there is a better Father waiting for you in heaven. You will be equally glad to go and stay with Him, would you not?" She knew what he desired in her response, and she affirmed that she wanted God's will.[23] And then, happy in spirit, he comforts her with his oft-quoted words, "Ah, thou dear Lenchen, thou wilt rise again, and shine forth as a star, nay, as a sun!"[24]

It would be difficult to imagine Katie saying such words as "happy in spirit"—or of such words being put into her mouth. Only those who have lost children can truly comprehend her complete and total devastation. God must have seemed distant or silent (if not cruel) as she stood helplessly by as her beloved daughter faded away.

In a letter to his close friend, Justus Jonas, Martin spoke from the heart in expressing his and Katie's feelings of desolation—desolation as though they were "experiencing death" themselves. But in a seeming effort to excuse his actual sorrow, he insisted that he and Katie should be rejoicing that she "escaped the power of the flesh, the world, the Turk, and the devil." In actuality, however, they were "unable to do this without crying and grieving in our hearts." He adds a comment that truly shows the depth of their grief: "The features, the words, and the movements of the living and dying daughter remain deeply engraved in the heart."[25]

What he confides next to Jonas, only Katie could have thought and Luther in his unabashed honesty could say: "Even the death of Christ . . . is unable to take this all away as it should. You, therefore, give thanks to God in our stead. For indeed God did a great work of grace when he glorified our flesh in this way. Magdalena had (as you know) a mild and lovely disposition and was loved by all."[26]

Hans, three years older than Magdalena, away at school in Torgau, had been summoned home when it seemed certain that his sister would not recover. In fact, he did not arrive home until after she had died, and he would not return, apparently at his mother's insistence, to continue his schooling at such a distance. In the ensuing years, he continued his schooling in Wittenberg, a decision that suggests Katie's strong influence. Luther, holding to the convention of the day, believed boys should be sent away from home for their studies.[27]

Understanding Katharina as a mother comes primarily through inference, that is, until she becomes a widow. It is then that we distinctly hear her voice and have a sense of certainty that her voice, though unrecorded, had always spoken with a deep primal love. She may not have always been the sweetest and tenderest of mothers, soothing every scratch on the knee, but she fiercely protected her children, even into their adult years.

Hans, born in 1526, the year after his parents married, had not yet celebrated his twentieth birthday when his larger-than-life father died in 1546. Although he "was obviously not too gifted intellectually," writes Martin Treu, Katie was bound and determined to get him through his course work at the University of Königsberg. Too strapped for money to pay for his education herself, she begged for money from various well-connected friends of her late husband. At university, he became a perpetual student of sorts, supported by Duke Albrecht of Prussia. And like others before and since, Hans, "in spite of his long-term studies, never held a position."[28]

Fourteen when his father died, Martin Jr. was the most deeply troubled of the five adult children. He remained in Wittenberg, close (at least in proximity) to his mother until she died in 1552, when he was nineteen. After that, his life began to go off the rails, and at the age of thirty-four, he died of alcoholism. Critics claimed Katie was too indulgent with the children, ever fearful that, out of her sight, one of them might fall ill and die.

Paul, never having been away from home on his own, was a mere boy of twelve when his father died. His adolescence lay ahead of him—a difficult time to be so soon fatherless. Yet he flourished in the decade that followed, earning a degree in medicine at the age of twenty-three.

His services were in demand by some of Germany's biggest names of the day: Duke Johann Friedrich of Saxony, Elector Joachim II of Brandenburg, and Elector August of Saxony.[29]

Youngest of the four surviving children, Margarethe was eleven at the time of her father's death, old enough to remember well when the family joined together in singing or sitting at table with students in the evening while her father held forth on various topics. She married a man of noble blood, and they lived together near Königsberg, where brother Hans was pursuing his career as a student. Like her mother, her pregnancies followed one after another. She died when she was in her mid-thirties of complications from her ninth childbirth.[30]

During the two decades of their marriage, Katie may have heard time and again her husband's views on motherhood. Perhaps she sometimes felt she did not measure up to his biblical standard. But it is more likely that much of what he said from his biblical and philosophical perspective did not really resonate with her—perhaps in one ear and out the other. "Bring the child forth and do it with all your might!" he had declared. "If you die in the process, then pass on over, good for you! For you actually die in a noble work and in obedience to God."[31] She obviously knew he was spouting off and didn't really mean what he was saying. He worried about her in every childbirth—and despaired that he was losing her in her last. Why would he say something so heartless? He obviously didn't mean such things.

"Men have broad chests and narrow hips, and for that reason they have more understanding than the women," Luther blabbed. Women "have narrow chests and wide hips and lower bodies, so that they ought to stay home and sit still in the house [and] keep house and bear and raise children."[32] This was said in 1531, when Katie, who hardly had a moment to sit still at all, was pregnant with her fourth child. What a lout!

But to Katie, Martin was a good husband who likely did not believe his own slurs against women. She was certain not only of his high personal regard for her but also of his esteem for women in general—esteem he drew directly from scriptural foundations. Motherhood was sacred in his mind, and there never had been a mother so worthy of honor as Katie—unless it were Eve. It is interesting how Luther's understanding of Eve evolved over the years. In the 1520s, he offered a standard negative portrait of her.

> [The younger Luther] faulted the first woman, "talkative and superstitious," for speaking with the serpent in the first place . . . He imagined her as a woman "simple," "weak," and "little," who had no business engaging in a "disputation" that from the outset was over her head; instead, she ought to have referred the devil's questions to the man, her superior . . .
>
> The younger Luther also connected Eve's failing in this case to her subjection to her husband's ecclesial authority.[33]

During his marriage to Katie, however, Luther's views changed. He looked at the text more dispassionately, his hermeneutic no longer shaped by a chauvinistic culture. Indeed, by the mid-1530s and early 1540s, he no longer saw Eve as Adam's inferior.

> The elder Luther—a married man who had fathered six children—offered a strikingly altered and imaginative portrayal of Eve, making her a great saint, a woman whose heroic faithfulness merited attention and emulation. Rather than weak, superstitious, and talkative, she is now a "heroic woman" . . . who engaged in conversations with the serpent because she recognized it instantly as one of the creatures over which she had been set, as a "partner in the rule" . . . with her husband, as ruler and keeper. She was, moreover, an excellent philosopher, "in no part, that is, neither in body nor in soul . . . inferior to her husband Adam."[34]

Eve is Adam's equal partner. For Luther to recognize that is striking in itself. But in a larger realm, Eve is far more than just Adam's equal.

She is *mother—mother of all living*. Eve was no mere incubator with wide hips. She was mother of *all living*—and she was a mother *all of her life*. So also Katie. Motherhood was far more than merely giving birth. With that understanding, Luther's rendition of Eve is extravagant—overspiritualizing what God had set in place as procreation. This is vintage Luther, not how Katie would have described the biblical scene. Nevertheless, she would have honored his effort to honor Eve and to honor her at the same time: "When Eve was brought unto Adam, he became filled with the Holy Spirit, and gave her the most sanctified, the most glorious of appellations. He called her Eva, that is to say, the mother of all. He did not style her wife; but simply mother—mother of all living creatures. In this consists the glory, and the most precious ornament of woman."[35]

Like Eve, Katie was styled by God and by her husband, not primarily as wife, but simply mother. "In this," Luther proclaimed, "consists the glory, and the most precious ornament of woman."

CHAPTER 8

"Morning Star of Wittenberg"

AT WORK BEFORE DAWN

I f you want someone to make a speech," quipped the former British prime minister Margaret Thatcher, "ask a man; if you want to get something done, ask a woman."[1] While this has often been said of the political realm, the same might also be said of the religious realm in general and of the Luthers in particular. Martin was known for his words, Katie for her work. In fact, Katie simply took for granted her role as a working mother—working both inside and outside the home.

Katie's daily work schedule, considering the lack of modern conveniences, is difficult to fathom. "Such a woman, who can find?" asks the author of Proverbs.[2] The obvious answer is that she cannot be found—unless we time-travel to the Black Cloister in sixteenth-century Wittenberg. The woman is none other than Katharina von Bora, as the writer of Proverbs describes:

> She selects wool and flax . . .
> She considers a field and buys it;
>> out of her earnings she plants a vineyard.
> She sets about her work vigorously;
>> her arms are strong for her tasks.

She sees that her trading is profitable,
  and her lamp does not go out at night . . .
She opens her arms to the poor . . .
Her husband is respected at the city gate . . .
She makes linen garments and sells them . . .
She watches over the affairs of her household
  and does not eat the bread of idleness.
Her children arise and call her blessed;
  her husband also, and he praises her.

Proverbs 31:13, 16–18, 20, 23–24, 27–28

The passage, however, seems altogether unreal, almost unnaturally clean—especially for what we expect to find in the Bible. Where is the pain in childbearing and the death of darling little ones? Where are the dirty diapers and the deadbeat boarders, the sharp words and sulking silences? In the real world of dirt and death, Katie matched the Proverbs 31 woman, and more. True, her lamp went out at night, but only for a few hours.

With six children of her own besides several orphans, motherhood, as we have seen, had become a full-time job. Add to that the adult relatives, students, and strangers, and it would seem as though she would have had no time for anything else. But she did. Truly Katie was a workaholic, in part because she could not depend on her husband for financial security. He was heading for old age when she had married him, and it would be left to her to provide for her children's future.

For most of her married life, Katie ran a boardinghouse. Except when her husband canceled their bill, young men paid her for room and board in her Black Cloister home. A bed-and-breakfast of today is no comparison. A term that best describes the general state of affairs is *bedlam*. Prince George of Anhalt, traveling to Wittenberg, was warned against staying at the Black Cloister, then "occupied by a motley crowd of boys, students, girls, widows, old women and youngsters." The writer lamented this primarily because of the "much disturbance" that interfered with the work of "the good man, the honorable father." The three-story structure had "forty rooms on the ground floor alone" and "was at times so chaotic that it is a wonder Luther was able to work."[3] In the midst of this bedlam, Katie soldiered on through the day as though it were normal.

She was in charge of all meals, housekeeping, bookkeeping, and laundry. When I was growing up, I had heard of old-time boardinghouses, and I now wish I would have asked more questions. Sharon Hunt offers insights:

> Boarding houses these days are indeed a relic. Their heyday was during the 19th and early 20th centuries . . . Many boarding houses in working-class areas were filthy and offered no privacy; sleeping in the same bed with strangers was not uncommon. Men with more money to spend could secure clean and private rooms, better food, and even hot water for shaving . . . [My grandmother] reluctantly opened her house to boarders when my grandfather injured his back and couldn't work for a long period. With five children under six, two sisters-in-law, and a mother-in-law as well as her husband and herself to feed, she had no choice.[4]

Katie's situation probably was not so different from that of Sharon's grandmother. Soon after she married Martin, she became pregnant—and then five more times in the next seven years. Martin could not claim a back injury for lack of funds, but as a matter of fact, he had no regular salary. Complicating the situation further was the rundown condition of the Black Cloister. But Katie, the skilled household manager, was able to stretch a small amount of money and at the same time curb her husband's fiscal carelessness.

That Martin referred to her as the "morning star of Wittenberg" was fitting.[5] As in her convent days, she rose at 4:00 a.m. or soon thereafter, though not for corporate worship. She rose before dawn to work, and she often kept at it until after dark. Six hours of sleep was a luxury. Most of the daily duties involved tiring manual labor, but there is no evidence that Katie would have considered the work disagreeable drudgery. In fact, at times we suspect we catch a glimpse of her merriment as she oversees the work in kitchen and garden.

It is reasonable to assume that her work ethic was shaped in the convent. In fact, since the age of five until her death, Katie had lived in a cloister—all but two years when she lived in private homes prior to marriage. Her marital home was the old red brick Black Cloister, named for the monks' black outerwear. But while living in this cloister, she was anything but cloistered. What kept her inside the walls was an ever-expanding workload. As she supervised the large household, she might have felt as though she had little more authority than did an abbess over a convent out of control. Like an abbess, she could not simply walk away, except for business trips out of town—though sometimes perhaps as much to get away from the grind. She most enjoyed the country air at her farms.

Martin Treu points out that Katie was far more than simply a *housewife*, that she was what we would consider today a "manager of a mid-sized business with low intensity production."[6] Surely she was far more than the sixteenth-century hausfrau, but a "mid-sized business" is misleading as well. Apart from nonprofits, there are few comparable businesses today that require such a diversity of skills and knowledge. But like many businesses, her boardinghouse and farms were not always money-making ventures. Nor is *boardinghouse* a truly accurate term because many of the residents did not pay for room and board.

Perhaps the best way to describe the staggering complexity of her work is as the corporate manager of a farm, garden, and monastery-medical hostel that housed extended family, travelers, and a significant number of hangers-on. All this while giving birth and taking in orphans. In fact, there were at times as many as thirty students boarding at the Black Cloister, paying for their keep in varying degrees.

Her workday was filled with a wide variety of specialized tasks, some not typically regarded as proper duties for a minister's wife. She was by all accounts one of the best brewmeisters in Wittenberg, a skill for which her husband was most appreciative. "I must remain longer here on account of the pious Prince," he lamented, while away for extended meetings. He missed her, but it was more than that: "Yesterday I had to take a nasty drink, and I do not like what is not good. I keep thinking what good wine and beer I have at home, as well as a beautiful wife, or shall I say lord? And you would do well to send me over my whole cellar of wine and a bottle of thy beer, or else I shall not be back before the new beer is ready."[7]

The farmwork in itself is a fascinating aspect of her life, though again she would have had farmhands working for her. And Luther himself enjoyed gardening and often helped in the planting and harvesting of large vegetable plots. She was no hobby gardener. Her garden supplied the family and residents with a variety of produce, including cucumbers, melons, squash, lettuce, cabbage, peas, beans, various herbs, and more. She was also in charge of the fields of grain needed for animal fodder, as well as wheat and barley fields critical for her brewing production. Beer was a staple at meals.

Besides the gardens, vineyard, orchard (apples, peaches, figs, and almonds), and fields, the complex included sheds and pastures. Katie kept chickens, ducks, goats, cattle, horses, swine, and honeybees, and she also oversaw a fishpond (stocked with perch, pike, trout, and carp). She was involved in every aspect of the work—even butchering livestock. We glean this information from various sources, including the letters of her husband. In a 1535 letter, Martin wrote that his lord Katie was busy planting crops, preparing pastures, and selling cattle.[8] In late May 1538, after a heavy rain, Luther commented to those at table how his abundant farm produce was a gift from God, as though God were raining down coins from heaven—coins in the form of cabbage, corn, onions, wine, and milk. And how do we show our gratitude, he sarcastically wondered—by crucifying God's only Son?[9]

It may have been raining corn and cabbage, all acquired for nothing—except, of course, for Katie's backbreaking work. And according to Martin, she worked circles around the servants. What her husband did not say in his letters was how absolutely furious she was when she realized that students were raiding her gardens or fruit trees during the night.[10] Her farming enterprises would continue to grow over the years, and by 1542, according to a tax statement, among all her other livestock, the farm boasted several sows and piglets, a goat and two kids, and fourteen head of cattle, yearling calves included.[11]

With rain and good weather, we can imagine this as a quaint Winslow Homer farm scene where Katie reigned supreme. But droughts and storms and harsh winters could quickly turn upside down all she had worked to accomplish. Marauding bandits and devastating plagues also wreaked havoc. Did she ever daydream about being back in the convent, disturbed only by predawn calls to prayer?

Some writers have suggested that Katie was known for the gift of hospitality. However, this would not likely have been the phrase she would have used. She welcomed people into her home in her often-abrupt manner, while efficiently caring for their needs. Noting her vitality, ingenuity, and hard work, writer and herbalist Sara Hall rightly sizes her up as "impossible to dismiss" with an aura of "sheer energy."[12] Indeed, sheer energy, perhaps more than any other phrase, sums up Katie von Bora.

Her generosity was probably most appreciated by those who had taken ill. She was "a master of herbs, poultices, and massage."[13] Son Paul, a medical doctor, regarded his mother not a *full* doctor like himself, but better than many as a *half* one. Luther, by some accounts, was the sickest patient of the Reformation, and she was his primary caregiver. Among her other ministrations, "she kept Luther from wine and gave him beer, which served as a sedative for insomnia and a solvent for the stone . . . When he was away from home, how he appreciated [and missed] her ministrations!"[14]

She was a proficient gardener, writes Steven Ozment, "gaining a reputation as an herbalist."[15] However, there is no record of herbal recipes or which plants she used from her garden and how she utilized them in healing. Herbal healing was widely practiced in the sixteenth century, even as early scientific medicine was gaining credence. Her gardening capabilities were no doubt drawn from the "great traditions of Monastic medicine," writes Sara Hall.[16] Indeed, German nuns were familiar with Hildegard von Bingen, whose writings included herbal recipes for virtually all identified ailments of the day. Outside the convent, most towns boasted of a healer—a woman specialist in folk medicine. Katie served in this capacity to her family and boarders, as well as to neighbors. "It is likely," writes Hall, "that she also cultivated the same herbs that were commonly cultivated in convents and monasteries: rue, sage, parsley, mint, wormwood, borage, aloe, rosemary, mugwort, pennyroyal, calendula (known as pot marigold), gladioli and basil."[17]

For those who love gardening, it is not difficult to imagine her flower beds in full bloom—including asters, roses, carnations, primrose, and lilies of every hue.[18] She took pride in her ability to grow saffron, a pricy spice that was difficult to acquire locally.

With more acquisitions of land, Katie's oversight of farming expanded, but all the while, her primary responsibility was inside the Black Cloister. Between pregnancies, she was burdened with household duties, which included procuring firewood to keep the large dwelling warm in the winter months. Some of the firewood came from her Zöllsdorf property. At this location (as well as others), she sometimes had conflicts with neighbors. Firewood was just one issue. The best timber was cut but was quickly snatched away by another buyer before Katie had sealed the deal. Some of this timber was to be sawn into planks for her renovations of the Black Cloister.[19]

The original structure was expanded in the late 1530s to accommodate the ever-growing household, and Katie, not surprisingly, was the general contractor for the large addition and the renovations that now included a bathhouse, brewery, and cattle stalls. Correspondence, according to Martin Treu, indicates that Katie was clearly in charge of decision making regarding renovations and use of space. She was the one who apparently situated the family's living space at the back of the building, where she could watch over the livestock and hired hands.[20]

A footnote to this expansion project sounds all too modern, though in this case there were no inspectors' surprise visits looking for code violations. Whether because of shoddy construction or failure to warn the residents with proper signage, the excavation for the new cellar collapsed. Word was that it might have killed both the Reformer and his wife. The death date for both would have been July 12, 1532.

Throughout the 1530s, students and supporters continued to vie for a space at table to listen to and record the words of the great teacher. But the house was also sometimes packed nearly to the rafters with those who simply needed lodging. Some stayed on for lengthy periods of time, including several of Martin's nieces and nephews. Those on Katie's side included not only her aunt who helped out with household management, but also Florian, her nephew. The numbers fluctuated, due to guests who arrived, often without warning, but Katie could count on around forty residents on a regular basis.[21]

There was no way the Black Cloister could be self-sufficient with so many residents, thus the continual increase of gardens and fields purchased and leased. This was not what Luther desired, but Katharina did what she had to do. She argued and won him over to her point of view, he reported, by "begging and crying."[22]

Yet even with the increase of gardens and fields, this land-hungry hausfrau was still not content. She contacted a distant relative about renting his much more expansive farm for only a year or two. She emphasized that she did not wish to purchase the farm, apparently to quash the town gossip that she would do virtually anything to increase her acreage. She was a hard bargainer, and apparently she was able to negotiate a low-cost lease. Although Martin had been required to sign off on the previous garden purchases, in this case, she did the letter writing and finalized the deal on her own.

But this lease had not satisfied Katie. She had long had her eye on a farm some two-day's distance away. The previously mentioned

Zöllsdorf farm was a property she knew well, having long been in the family and most recently owned by her brother. Had she been one of her father's sons, she might have held ownership years earlier. But now her brother was financially unable to keep it. We can only imagine how desperate she was to purchase the land for herself before strangers grabbed it up, even though she knew very well that the property (which included buildings in disrepair) would require significant improvements. But more than that, how could she be serious, considering the distance and the high price? The idea was preposterous. The year was 1540. She had a houseful of kids, her youngest being five years old.

This time, however, her husband was on board. He had begun to feel as though Wittenberg was no longer his home. Enemies seemed to be multiplying by the month. Here on this farm south of Leipzig, he might be able to find some peace and quiet. That this acquisition of property would keep his wife away from Wittenberg for long periods of time, however, was not his concept of the ideal marriage. But Katie was persistent.

While it is true she wanted the family land in part for sentimental reasons, she was also motivated by a belief ground into her genes from ancient times that land ownership is to be equated with financial security. Whether her various transactions were all equally wise is a matter debated by historians. But considering the times, marked by bad weather, war, and repeated plagues, security was not easily attained—not even with land. Yet the Luthers, at least while Martin was alive, were far more stable financially than were other families in Wittenberg. The primary difference was that the other families had no hardworking wheeler-dealer to turn poverty into prosperity. "The credit for their economic expansion," writes Martin Treu, "is finally due to Katharina alone."[23]

One would imagine that building up the family estate with land acquisitions would be enough for a woman overseeing the household and farms. But if Katie appears self-serving in acquiring land that her husband is less than enthusiastic about, we dare not forget her efforts on his behalf in dealing with publishers to see that his works were printed and widely circulated. On one occasion, when he was away, Luther sent word home. "Katharina was ordered to march into the [print] shop, remove the manuscript, and reassign it to Rhau," another printer.[24] It was an assignment, we can imagine, she might have relished. More than her husband, she made a conscious effort to acquire rightful remuneration even for her husband's spoken words. On one occasion, when Katie learned that students were selling their notes taken at table while her husband was speaking, she insisted that he should start charging them. He retorted that he had been teaching for no remuneration for three decades, and he was *not* going to start asking for money now.[25]

Martin's opposition to Katie's selling his spoken words seems to have been settled, but she nevertheless continued to fight for his financial rights. She also was keen on serving him in his work as professor, always prepared to throw a party if his profession required it. A typical occasion is apparent from one of his letters acknowledging newly awarded doctorates to two of his friends. Katie is presumed to be head cook, who will be prepared to stir up a fine stew, sparrows and all. And if the stew is less than tasty, who cares while consuming steins of her best-brewed beer:

> I hope you have received the letters and disputations, with the directions, sent from a very incompetent person, to teach you what to say at the ceremony of conferring doctors' degrees; and now our head cook, Kathie, begs you will . . . send us birds and what you can find in your region of the air . . . But send us no ravens, but sparrows in any number . . . and if you can get a hare, or shoot anything for nothing, or purchase some vegetables, then send these also, for the principal thing is that you all get something to eat, for one must not depend on beer alone, of which my Kathie has brewed fourteen tuns, in which she has put thirty-two bushels of malt to suit my taste.[26]

Luther continues by giving an overview of the dismal political situation and then concludes with his standard optimism and good humor about his "head cook":

> But Christ lives, so let us rejoice even amid the rage of devils and men, enjoying the good things of life, till they come to a miserable end, especially if you confer your delightful society upon us, with your captives, who, under the sway of the head cook, will be consigned to the captivity of the pot. My Kathie and all greet you respectfully.[27]

Katie's brewing has caught the attention of many modern-day microbrewers. And German brewers are particularly proud of having her as a part of their heritage and include that fact in their advertising for light beers: "Who would have believed that light beers have a 450-year history?" the Würzburger Hofbräu commercial description reads. "The beer brewed by ["the health-conscious" and "gifted brewer"] Katharina von Bora was very light, under two percent . . . The reduction in alcohol content means . . . easily digestible 40% less alcohol and calories compared to . . . Pilsner Full beer flavor."[28]

While hosting large gatherings amid all her other work, Katie found time for informal counseling. She was no therapist—or even a self-appointed life coach—but she did counsel guests who were in need of her advice. In fact, as early as 1528, she had opened the Black Cloister to a runaway nun, Duchess Ursula of Munsterberg. Like Katie, Ursula was of noble heritage and had been placed in a convent as a young child—in her case, as an orphan. Although the Magdalen convent was a three-day journey away, and Ursula had frail health, she was determined to find her way to Wittenberg, where she and two other runaway nuns would find a safe house with Katie and the great Reformer. Ursula, accompanied by Dorothy and Margaret, had simply slipped out of the convent gate and walked to a nearby town—no horse-drawn herring wagon in the dead of night. Soon after they arrived in Wittenberg, Martin Luther left to attend meetings.

The four former nuns would have had a lot in common, all of them having escaped the territory of the much-feared Duke George. What a conversation it must have been—a satisfied, settled, and celebrated runaway nun encouraging three others who must have felt out of place in the world outside. It is not difficult to imagine Katie putting them at ease and enjoying some insider grievances and jokes.

Unlike Katie, Ursula was a writer and was eager to tell her story in a tract—her story of why she could no longer live under the rule of a convent. Although a convent life that required fasting and disruptions in sleep had taken a toll on her health, she framed her arguments for leaving in theological terms. Her words resonate with Martin's, whose tracts had influenced her to escape. Here she insisted that faith in Christ was one's only hope for salvation and that the claim that monastic vows, like baptism, cleanse from sin was nothing short of blasphemy.[29]

Duke George, still stung by the escape of Katie and eleven other nuns from a convent under his rule five years earlier, was furious about the escape of Ursula, particularly because she was a duchess from a prominent family. No less angry was he about what he considered vile propaganda published in a tract with Luther's postscript. What was he to do? Send troops to Wittenberg and arrest her? Ursula bided her time, and after two months, she and her sister nuns sought shelter elsewhere, where they were provided a more permanent safe haven. Ursula's poor health, however, persisted, and she died in 1534, leaving all her worldly goods to her dear sister nun Dorothy.

Ursula, Dorothy, and Margaret were certainly not the only ones who profited from Katie's ministry of kindness. Like the Proverbs 31 woman, Katie opened her arms to the poor and sick—and not just to runaway nuns. Katharina could be counted on in times of need, but she never lost her focus in life. Her first priority was her husband—a teacher, preacher, writer, conversationalist who drew students by the dozens to the Black Cloister. There was no competition between Katie and him. She supported him wholeheartedly, knowing that students were certainly not gathering around to hear her "table talk." Her husband was the draw—a valuable commodity. As such, her home was a for-profit business. Students would not be freeloaders under her watch. Katie knew her place. She was wife, mother, and breadwinner.

Amid all her relatives, friends, and boarders, Katie maintained a tight ship. "She often seems grasping and even petty in her quest for money, and we have many hints that Wittenbergers did not like her," writes Richard Marius. She was a hard taskmaster, not only with servants but Luther as well. He was known for his generosity, while Katie "kept her eye on the bottom line."[30]

There's an ancient folktale I learned as a child about a husband who complains because his work in the fields is much harder than his wife's work around the house. So one day she suggests they switch chores. She finishes all the work in the fields, and when she arrives home late in the day, she discovers everything has gone awry. What a mess, including her husband who has, through a series of mishaps, fallen headfirst down the chimney into a pot of porridge!

Katie might have laughed at such a tale, but it hardly related to her daily routine. She did the work of both husband and wife: feeding the pigs and chickens, milking cows, churning butter, grinding meal, cleaning house, washing clothes, preparing meals as well as working the fields—all this much appreciated by the husband, who spent his days preaching, teaching, debating, attending meetings, writing books, playing with children, and talking at table. Is there another German folktale to be found in this story? If so, it needs to be recorded for posterity.

"Hew an Obedient Wife Out of Stone"

PUSHING GENDER BOUNDARIES

The Reformation paved the way for gender equality, opening doors for women in ministry and public life, and women rose to the occasion, throwing aside their shackles. True or false? Or did this new Protestant faith close doors? Was the era of the great ruling abbess beginning to fade?

"Did the Protestant reformers somehow promote the cause of women in church or society?" asks Mickey Mattox. "One source in this debate is the theology of Martin Luther and his own life and practice, especially in relationship with his wife Katharina von Bora. Luther has sometimes been portrayed as a champion of women's rights in the church, but his authoritative voice has also been invoked as a final bulwark against 'feminist' claims."[1]

I'll never forget teaching a church history course at Fuller Theological Seminary in the early 1990s. It was a large class, mostly men but nearly a dozen women as well. I had not actually noticed a gender divergence as we were working our way through the medieval church. Both women and men seemed to be fully engaged. But suddenly, things changed the day we arrived at Martin Luther and 1517—for me as much as anyone else. I was in a celebratory mood.

When the morning clock struck nine, I had the students stand and sing "A Mighty Fortress Is Our God" as a few stragglers snuck in. The men's voices filled every square inch of the room and out into the halls. If women were singing, their voices were overpowered. Lecture and discussion followed.

But as tone-deaf as I was, I *still* didn't get it. I didn't notice a certain sullenness among the women—not until the next day, not until after most of the women had time to talk among themselves. Initially, they bided their time. Then I said something about the Reformation opportunities for women. Only then did they start unloading on me, almost as though they had their own ninety-five theses written out and prepared for the moment. I was taken aback, naive as I was then. Didn't we all march to the same drummer and make a triumphal entry into the Reformation?

One woman stood alone, opposing the other female students. She jumped in at every opportunity to tell about her own transition from the darkness of Catholicism to the light of truth. But I let neither her nor the defensive Protestant men in the class hold the floor. It was critical to let these women's voices bring balance. And I quickly realized they had rightly toned down my triumphalism. Perhaps if I had been lecturing on Katie von Bora, these students might have reacted differently, especially if I had thrown out some of Luther's quips on marriage: "I am an inferior lord, she the superior; I am Aaron, she is my Moses."[2]

It is important to note, however, that serious degradation of women was standard among both Catholics and Protestants. "Between 1487 and 1623," writes Gerhild Williams, "women's place in the society of Northern Europe, in the family, and even within herself became increasingly precarious . . . Too deeply had the polemics about her physical, mental, and spiritual inferiority affected the minds of both men and women."[3]

Space here does not permit a serious discussion of the Catholic versus Protestant gender debate as it relates to the sixteenth century.

Suffice it to say that my own position today is much more nuanced than it was a quarter century ago in the early 1990s. Moreover, since then and since the ascension of Pope Francis, there has been a healthy, widespread warming trend between Catholics and Protestants.

But a celebration of the five-hundred-year anniversary of 1517 brings me back to the real advances for women brought about by the Reformation. The words of many of the medieval abbesses often seem stilted. Indeed, women's voices were too often authenticated by visions from on high. I want to hear their own voices, not their claimed directives from God—though, of course, these *were* their own voices. Protestant Reformers—men and women—supported their religious claims with their interpretations of Scripture, and they argued among themselves. Argula von Grumbach railed against Catholics, Katherine Zell against other Reformers, with no need to trot out special revelations from God. But among monastic women, visionary experiences frequently transported them into priestly roles the church denied them, giving them, in the words of historian Carolyn Bynum, "direct authorization to act as mediators to others"[4]—also giving them a unique role in defining church tradition.

How, for example, is the immaculate conception of Mary (that she was born and ever remained sinless), to be believed? If the doctrine was actually confirmed by God in visions to both Birgitta of Sweden and Catherine of Siena, there can be no protest. But the *Protest*-ant perspective demanded scriptural support and offered ordinary individuals a greater sense of empowerment to speak their own minds on religious issues. Women joined in, talking back to religious authorities—and their husbands as well.

Until I began my research on this book, I had on the tip of my tongue the three great women Reformers, should anyone have asked. I identified them, beginning with the oldest: Argula von Grumbach, Katherine Zell, and Renée of Ferrara. They were serious religious protesters, but Katie was not one of them. I have since concluded, however, that in a very significant way, Katie contributed more to the Protestant movement than all three of them combined. Without them, the sixteenth-century Reformation would have certainly lost vitality, but the content and form would have changed little. Not so if Katie were missing. Yet these women added flavor and zest that most historians have failed to detect.

Seven years older than Katie, Argula stepped to the fore in the early 1520s with boldness and Bavarian noble blood to defend those who followed Martin Luther. As we have seen, she appeared before the Diet of Nuremberg and also wrote letters and tracts defending the Reformed faith in Germany. In doing so, her husband's court status was in jeopardy, and she was accused of neglecting her children and risking her own life. She had clearly violated her expected role as a woman.

Katherine Schütz Zell grew up in a large prosperous family in Strasbourg, where she acquired a first-rate education. Unlike Katie, she was not forced into a religious life. In fact, with no apparent prodding, she became deeply interested in spiritual and theological matters as a young child. Then in her mid-twenties, she sensed a call to be a minister's wife—perhaps the first such call in Christian history. In the words of Elsie Anne McKee, she "was convinced that she was called to marry Matthew Zell as an expression of her faith in God and her love for others."[5] Early Protestants, unlike Catholics, offered no opportunities for single women in full-time ministry, but as a pastor's wife, Katherine found many opportunities for ministry in Strasbourg. After her husband's death, she was on the defensive about her own role as a preacher in the church.

Renée of Ferrara was a princess who married the grandson of Pope Alexander VI, Ercole II d'Este—a political marriage, to be sure. That popes had children and grandchildren was a fact of life, one that Luther harped on repeatedly. She was more than ten years younger than Katie, and married at eighteen, three years after Katie had married in 1525. More than age, however, separated them. Renée was royalty, and her Protestant connections were with John Calvin, whose Reformation in Geneva did not begin until the mid-1530s, nearly two decades after Luther's. Like Argula and Katherine, Renée was committed to Reformed teachings, and like them, she was accused of stepping out of line as a woman.

Although Katie never spoke out about gender inequality, her assumption of equality was more than equal to theirs. But as we consider her alongside them, a significant difference was their marital situations. Argula and Renée, in their commitment to the Reformation, took serious risks in their being married to opponents of reform. Indeed, both of them faced grave consequences in an era when the death penalty was often as close as a stake, a pile of kindling, and a lighted torch. Katie and Katherine, on the other hand, were married to Reformers who were supportive of their wives, though in very dissimilar ways. Katherine, whose only two children died as infants, was active working alongside her husband, writing tracts and hymns and heading various humanitarian ministries, while Katie was consumed with household and business enterprises. Neither husband, however, outwardly supported gender equality.

Of the four husbands, Martin Luther was the most vocal in his defense of male headship. And among the women, Katie took female equality most for granted and overtly acted on that principle. Indeed, these four women illustrate gender issues that have arisen, both then and now. An interesting aspect of equality among evangelicals is the two-pronged nature of the discussion. One is theory versus practice; the other is ministry versus marriage. The primary issue for Argula, Katherine, and Renée related to equality in ministry and church matters. All three of them ran up against roadblocks when they overstepped accepted boundaries. Katie, however, had no aspirations to publicly defend the faith, as did Argula and Katherine, or to vote at meetings of synod, as did Renée.

For Katie, the issue related to male headship in marriage. Unlike her sister Reformers, however, we never observe her defending equality. Martin might pontificate as much as he liked on the subject, but she had work to do and decisions to make. And pontificate he did, whether

135

at church or at table. Like many ministers, he was quite capable of pulling rules from the Bible where none existed. Preaching from Genesis on one occasion, he concluded that the woman must submit to the man, particularly a wife to husband. The wife was to submit to her husband's authority and to dwell wherever he chose. Only a foolish woman would seek to skirt such admonitions. A woman is not capable of decision making and is thus utterly unsuitable for leadership or for filling any level of governing positions—"unable to govern cities and territories, etc." Although, as is true in Scripture, she may give advice to him, but only rarely.[6]

His first claim almost seems laughable, considering the Genesis 2 directive: " . . . a man leaves his father and mother and is united to his wife." And also his claim that women giving advice is rare—where does he get that? It happens time and again in Holy Scripture, particularly in Genesis. None of the great patriarchs had particularly submissive wives. Not Abraham. Not Isaac. Not Jacob. Indeed, when we survey women of the Hebrew Bible, they often act more like Jochebed, Miriam, Jael, Tamar, Abigail, or Gomer—hardly a harem of submissive and fawning women. And governing "cities and territories"? Didn't Deborah govern more effectively than any other judge in Israel?

Some of Luther's statements are not dated, and we can forgive him for being ignorant of marriage relationships before he tied the knot with Katie. And some of his positions gradually changed, particularly, as we have seen, in his assessment of Eve and her place alongside Adam. But many of his rants are so excessive and absurd that no excuses are valid. Some of Luther's statements are plainly chauvinistic and shocking to our ears today. Even a mature woman, he claimed, is weaker in both body and spirit than man—not even a full adult, but a "half-child," a half-woman. So the husband, like a father, ends up caring for a girl.[7]

What was he thinking? There is no evidence that his mother, who carried a big stick when it came to child discipline, had a weak spirit or was in any way childlike. Nor was Barbara, the wife of his artist friend, Lucas Cranach—and certainly not Katharina von Bora. Analyzing such gender slurs, one might imagine Martin Luther was unusually insecure about his own manliness.

How did Katie deal with such slurs? She appears to have simply gone her own way, and as such she stands as a compelling model for women today, whether facing discrimination in marriage or ministry. Sure, her husband touted male headship, but that stance seemed to have little to do with how he structured their marriage. And Luther? For all his celebrity and capable leadership of the German Reformation, he was a weak man, both physically and emotionally. Katie knew that better than anyone else. Her strength was in inverse proportion to his weakness.

One does wonder why Martin felt it necessary to prop himself up alongside Katie. He conceded that he was glad to give her the run of the house, but insisted he would never agree to "letting himself be ruled by her," insisting that such marriages were "the vice of the age."[8] Yet he admits that his own household was beset with the vice of the age: "My wife can persuade me anything she pleases, for she has the government of the house in her hands alone. I willingly yield the direction of domestic affairs, but wish my rights to be respected. Women's rule never did any good."[9]

Well, one might ask, if women's rule never did any good, why would Martin let her rule such a large household? And that is exactly what Katie did. It never would have occurred to her to try to write his sermons or tell him how to respond to a theological opponent (although she did persuade him to respond to Erasmus when he was reluctant to do so). Such was not in the realm of her interest or expertise. But regarding the household matters and all the properties and business enterprises that so significantly affected their marriage, she ruled. She was capable—anything but a childlike wife. And he, for the record, was the one with the weaker spirit. For sure.

On one occasion while Luther was conversing with Justus Jonas and another friend in his garden, Jonas lamented "that the women were becoming our masters" (perhaps with Katie in mind). The other friend, a Torgau town councilor, added "that it was indeed, alas!" Luther, drawing from his own experience agreed: "But we have to give in, otherwise we would have no peace."[10] When I read that, I couldn't help smiling. But there is no reason to imagine that Katie was Martin's master because she wanted to rule over him. Rather, she was decisive, efficient, and mentally stable, and in order to properly conduct household and financial affairs, she took charge. It was as simple as that—a very modern perspective on how to work out a mutually satisfying marriage.

There were any number of Luther's colleagues and wags about town who were no fans of Katie and were not afraid to say so. These included Conrad Cordatus, Caspar Cruciger, and Johannes Agricola, who, according to Ernst Kroker, "tell us unanimously that she had a power over him like no one else."[11] In fact, Cordatus made derogatory comments about Katie in his *Table Talk* notes. He was especially annoyed by "her long speeches" and her "interrupting her husband in the middle of the finest conversations if the food was going to get cold."[12] On one occasion, when Luther humorously welcomed a guest, saying, "Indulge a meek host for he is obedient to the lady," Cordatus noted with exasperation, "This is most certainly true!"[13] Philip Melanchthon referred to Katie as the *despoina* (the Latin root for "despot") of the house.[14]

Some have suggested it was Katie who spurred Martin in his attacks on others. But in fact, the opposite was true. On one occasion, she pleaded with him to work things out with Johannes Agricola, a one-time friend whom Luther now regarded an enemy because he had come to devalue the law in favor of grace. "In vain Frau Elsa and Frau Katie tried to intervene," writes Kroker. "The urgent pleas of the one and the tears of the other were not able to change his mind."[15] Luther insisted Agricola must retract his theological position before their friendship could continue, a decision that negatively impacted Katie's friendship with Elsa.

As to women's equality in ministry, Luther insisted that women were not allowed to preach. When some of the radicals permitted women in the pulpit, he deemed the idea preposterous. A woman's place was in the home, not in public affairs: "Women talk a lot, but they have no understanding, and when they attempt to speak about serious things, they speak foolishness."[16] Again, such language does not square with his attitude toward women in the public square—particularly if they were working for the Reformation cause. Argula von Grumbach was praised for her courage—she alone standing up for Reformed tenets amid much persecution. And Martin worked alongside Ursula of Münsterberg as she prepared her tract.

Katherine Schütz Zell had used self-deprecating terminology to open doors, insisting she had as much right to speak the word of God as did Balaam's ass. And she was not speaking for herself alone. Though only "a splinter from [his] rib," she had the support "of that blessed man Matthew Zell."[17] Katherine's marriage to Matthew in December 1523 was shocking to the people of Strasbourg, even as it would be more than a year later when Katie married Martin. When news spread of the Luther nuptials, Katie seems to have remained silent, while Martin fired back at critics. Not so Katherine Zell. She was furious that her marriage would be seen as a scandal. With her written words, she claimed the moral high ground, insisting that clerical marriage was far superior to the common practice of a priest living with his mistress, or worse, seducing one woman after another.

Was Matthew upset with Katherine for her failure to keep house? Did he beat her for stepping out of line? There were rumors that he did, and she was livid. No, she was not neglecting her household duties—"I have never had a maid," and "as for thrashing me, my husband and I have never had an unpleasant 15 minutes."[18] And what of Martin and Katie? Speaking of a man who lost his freedom when he married a wealthy woman, Martin said, "I am luckier, for when Katie gets saucy she gets nothing but a box on the ear."[19] This seems to have been no more than an offhand effort at humor. A house full of students, quills in hand, would have noted a boxing on the ear and scribbled it down for posterity. That Katie was saucy was clearly in the record.

Saucy women, however, knew that even if they were not boxed on the ear or thrashed, they would be severely criticized. After Argula became famous for her challenges to Catholic doctrine, one Professor Hauer attacked her mercilessly. In one single sermon on December 8, he let loose, calling her, among other things, a "female devil," a "female desperado," a "wretched and pathetic daughter of Eve," an "arrogant devil," a "fool," a "heretical bitch," and "shameless whore."[20] Among other claims, she had the audacity to suggest that the Virgin Mary was an ordinary woman, not, as Catholics argued, *Theotokos*, the *Mother of God*.

That Katie was not typically interested in the fine points of theology would hardly have meant she spoke foolishness, as Martin sometimes implied. Indeed, she may have regarded some of his theological nitpicking as little more than foolishness.

Luther's most oft-quoted putdown of Katie, repeated endlessly by his biographers, relates to what he perceived as her foolishness. He liked to tell how on one occasion when he was concentrating on his writing, Katie was nearby "prattling." And then she innocently asked, "Herr Doctor, is the Hochmeister the Margrave's brother?" Luther turned this simple question into a joke at Katie's expense. Margrave Albrecht of Brandenburg had among his many titles "Hochmeister" ["Supreme Master"].[21] She had no doubt heard the last name with different titles, assuming two different people were involved. Oh, how stupid of her, how foolish—foolish enough for him to demean her and thus womanhood in general.

It is doubtful that Martin Luther, unlike Matthew Zell, could have ever appreciated a wife who was, in fact, theologically literate. It was one thing for Katie to challenge him on household, agricultural, and money matters, and quite another if she had taken him on in biblical exegesis and theology. But stand up to him she did, and apparently with great regularity. "I must have patience with . . . [my] Katie von Bora," he said, which means "my whole life is nothing else but mere patience."[22] On another occasion, he remarked at table, "If I ever have to find myself a wife again, I will hew myself an obedient wife out of stone."[23]

Such was the situation from the very beginning of their marriage. Indeed, she immediately took charge of the household and more. According to Nicolaus von Amsdorf, Martin did not wish to live in the rambling Black Cloister. In fact, there was much to commend in the comfortable homes of his colleagues. But Katie was convinced the cloister could become a money-making business. Why shouldn't she collect fees from student lodging rather than a local inn? She is quoted as saying, "I have to get the doctor used to my different way so that he does it the way I want it."[24]

Luther would have argued throughout his marriage that his wife did not rule the roost, as some had alleged. In fact, in defending male headship in all areas of life, Luther made his position clear.

> The rule remains with the husband, and the wife is compelled to obey him by God's command. He rules the home and the state, wages war, defends his possessions, tills the soil, builds, plants, etc. The woman on the other hand is like a nail driven into the wall. She sits at home . . . Just as the snail carries its house with it, so the wife should stay at home and look after the affairs of the household, as one who has been deprived of the ability of administering those affairs that are outside and that concern the state. She does not go beyond her most personal duties.[25]

Many who defend male headship quote these lines and others. But Luther's actions always spoke louder than his words, and in his private correspondence with his wife, it is obvious their marriage was one of mutuality—one of amazing equality for sixteenth-century Germany. A letter written when he was away from home in 1540 is an example of how deferential he was to her, while at the same time chiding her for not writing to him:

Dear maiden Kethe, gracious lady of Zölsdorf (and whatever else Your Grace is called)! I submissively give you Your Grace to know that things are going well with me here. I eat like a Bohemian and drink like a German. God be thanked, Amen . . .

I have received the children's letters . . . but from Your Grace I have received nothing. The fourth letter [this one] would you, God willing, answer for once with your own hand . . .

Martinus Luther.

Your sweetheart [from Weimar, July 1540][26]

Their marriage of equality is also apparent in the frequent example of mutual decision making. In a letter written in September 1541 from Wittenberg to Katie in Zöllsdorf, he again chides her for her lack of communication when she was away—for not writing back to him and advising him on how to proceed on certain matters. In the same letter, he tells her to come home but not before making land sales and purchases on her own. There was little time to waste, due to dangerous political and military developments.[27] Here he appears to be exercising his rightful male headship, but his very general orders are to sell and purchase—and to send *him* instructions. He is certainly not micromanaging her. And if we were to overhear them in a face-to-face discussion, she would be interacting with him as an equal. His telling her to come home is not to get her to buckle under his authority, but because he is worried sick about her well-being.

It is true that all these matters concern issues unrelated to church and theology. But before we put the clamp on her in this area of the religious arena, we have further words from the great Wittenberg professor himself. He wrote to Katie in the summer of 1540, addressing her in his usual affectionate terms: "To my dearly beloved Kate, Doctora Lutherin, and Lady of the New Pig Market . . . I want, obediently, to let Your Grace know that I am in good health here."[28] The message, however, relates to business, but by no means the usual household, farming, and financial matters. His startling assignment for her comes in connection with a letter discussing the matter of a pastoral appointment in the town of Greussen. What follows is no less than shocking. He wants her—"a wise woman and doctora"—to sit on the committee of three men in the decision-making process. He had extraordinary confidence in her, one who was not only "prudent," but also one who would "make a better choice" than apparently anyone else he might call on.[29]

For all Luther's bluster on matters of women in authority in civic life and in the church, and for all his derision and teasing, when he needed someone he could trust with sound judgment, he would break his own rules and call on Katie.

He often addressed her in letters using the masculine term for lord (*dominus*) rather than the feminine *domina*. Indeed, he loved to play with words, teasing her by calling her Kette rather than Kethe, the former meaning "chains." He acknowledged he was being kept in chains by his beloved wife.[30] Both Martin and Katie must be credited for this remarkable relationship. She because she indeed was confident, secure, and levelheaded and had proven to be a woman fully equal to Martin. And he because he was secure enough to accept her as such. Sure, he pontificated and put forth the party line of male headship and women's obedience. But in their own relationship, she stood tall beside him, perhaps a bit too "proud" for his taste, but never cowering.

Katie von Bora, like Abigail Smith two centuries later, was ahead of her time. Both were mothers of six children and married to revolutionary leaders who are today celebrated historical figures. Abigail was the wife of John Adams, revolutionary provocateur and second president of the United States. Katie and Abigail kept the home fires burning while their larger-than-life husbands hammered out documents and traveled for high-level debates and planning sessions. Like Katie, Abigail was often blunt in expressing her views and thus disliked by those who thought she overstepped gender boundaries. Katie would have appreciated Abigail's chutzpah. Had Katie been first lady of the American Revolution, we can imagine her voicing opinions as controversial as those of Abigail. In her oft-quoted letter of March 31, 1776, to her husband, John, who was serving at the time as Massachusetts representative to the first Continental Congress, Abigail wrote:

> Remember the ladies and be more generous and favorable to them than your ancestors. Do not put such unlimited power into the hands of the husbands. Remember all men would be tyrants if they could. If particular care and attention is not paid to the ladies, we are determined to foment a rebellion, and will not hold ourselves bound by any laws in which we have no voice or representation.[31]

Determined to foment a rebellion. Katie and Abigail were sisters in spirit. There is a footnote to Abigail's story that surely would have tickled Katie—Katie, who proposed to Nicolaus von Amsdorf to marry either him or Luther. Tradition in Abigail's day (as throughout most of recorded history) required a young man to seek permission of his sweetheart's father before proposing to her. When a young man proposed to Abigail's granddaughter Caroline before asking permission from Caroline's father (Abigail's son), Abigail thought it was only proper that Caroline, not her father, make the decision. Her position on this point was without qualification: "I shall maintain the supremacy of the ladies in this matter."[32]

CHAPTER 10

"*Stop Worrying, Let God Worry*"

WORRYWART OF WITTENBERG

H ostile natural and supernatural forces, mysterious and deadly epidemics, violent and malevolent fellow human beings, accidental or intentional fires—all haunted the imaginations and daily lives of early modern people," writes Joel Harrington. This "precariousness of life," however, belongs to all ages. "Fear and anxiety are woven into the very fabric of human existence. In that sense they link all of us across the centuries."[1]

But not all individuals are equally beset by fear and anxiety. "I am rich," Luther once said, "God has given me my nun and three children: what care I if I am in debt, Katie pays the bills."[2] Katie, however, did worry. Fear and anxiety were woven into her very existence.

I resonate with Katie on so many levels and have come to realize we have much in common. I fantasize about spending a week or two with her. We would surely not sit around and talk. We would work. She too often viewed her servants as slackers. Not so with me. I could keep pace with her, no matter what the task, and our personalities would easily mesh. We both know how to talk back to a husband and to accomplish an awful lot in one day. We both know how cold an outhouse can be on a bitter winter morning. We know how to milk cows by hand, tend chickens, and wield an axe. True, I have no capability of brewing beer (as much as my husband would prefer that over my talking back), but in so many ways, she's my sister. And not just because of our barbarian German ancestors. We are both worrywarts. In fact, on that score, we mirror each other. When it comes to worrying, I'm a champion. I can worry faster and more efficiently than anyone I know. And no one but Katie would have a clue what I'm talking about. I unconsciously rank by number my revolving worries—worries that are always circling back in one form or another.

Katie worried about money and crops and weather and plagues and house renovations and children. But more than anything else, she worried about Martin. Indeed, she was sick with worry in February 1546—and for good reason. His letter from Eisleben, dated February 7, chided her: "Leave me alone with your worry. I have a better comforter than you and all the angels. He lies in the manger and at the breast of a virgin, but at the same time sits at the right hand of God the Almighty Father. Therefore be at peace!"[3] Eleven days later, he was dead.

My son is now in his forties, and I still haven't stopped worrying about him. What's wrong with me? If I confessed this to him, he'd be furious. Sure, he would say, maybe twenty-five years ago—when I learned from a friend that he was in the ER after a serious auto accident, the result of bad decisions. Maybe even a dozen years ago, he would say, but now? Get over it. Leave me alone, and let God do the worrying. I can't, though most of the time these days he's far lower on my list than he was in his late teens.

It's February as I write. Income taxes are high on the list. So is flooding. We live in a flood plain, and spring floods are the norm. Kayaking back and forth to our "island" home is not a problem, but what about when the river decides to come right inside the house, as it did in the spring of 2013? So I worry. And I worry about our cottage, which is also on the river, more easily flooded than our house. I worry about squirrels getting into the attic of the cottage, causing our renter sleepless nights. I worry about our vehicle breaking down when we're traveling, now with nearly three hundred thousand miles on it; I worry about the duct tape that's holding the rear lights from falling off. I worry that John might die someday and leave me a widow. I worry about myself, that I might be diagnosed with brain cancer—or worse yet, Alzheimer's. And so it goes.

Katie's worries were not frivolous. She could easily list terrible tragedies—personal and public—that could be repeated in one form or another without warning. They were as real as the cancer diagnosis and death my husband faced with his two dearly departed wives. But does he worry? Not particularly. For Katie (and myself), however, worry is an ever-present shadow.

One wonders if Katie's worry might have begun as a very young child. Think of a five-year-old whose mother dies and is soon expected to make room for a stepmother and a bunch of kids in a house already too crowded. How would she react? Is anything in life permanent? What will happen next? She would find out soon enough. The wagon is headed for an uncertain future filled with strangers and setbacks. The saddest story of Martin's childhood is being thrashed by his mother for stealing a nut.[4] More than one writer in the field of psychohistory has wondered what permanent scars Mommy Dearest might have inflicted. Luther is the perfect subject for such psychoanalysis because of his excesses and idiosyncrasies. In contrast, Katie seems almost too normal.

Prior to their marriage, when Martin accused Katie of being proud, one wonders if such a trait might have actually been a well-developed defense mechanism. Katie alone was responsible for the course of her life. Unlike her husband, she does not appear to have had a strong sense of God's sovereign will over her life. She was in charge of getting things done in the large household and in making decisions that would ensure financial security—collecting rent from boarders, buying and selling land. God was not going to do that. She was in charge of keeping her children and husband healthy—and alive—projects not always successful, despite her best efforts. And so she worried.

We cannot assume that worries were necessarily a negative factor in her capable daily routine. In fact, Graham Davey writes in *Psychology Today* that "there is good evidence that in most people worrying is associated with a problem-focused coping style (that is, a willingness to approach and deal with problems), and it's also associated with an information-seeking coping style." Most people admit to worrying but say that it helps them "think constructively" about problems they are facing.[5]

The record of Katie's activities and accomplishments would lead us to believe that much of her worry could be listed in the constructive category. But even constructive worry can cause sleep loss, and she had no sleep to spare. Household matters and farmwork amid the perils of bad weather would have been enough cause for worry, but when the terror of the times was added, a weaker woman might have suffered a breakdown. Unlike in North America today, where plagues and wars and terrorism are often a world away, her world of anxieties were only a village or a room away: floods, famine, bitter winters, plague, pestilence, lawlessness, war. Added to such normal fears in the sixteenth century was that an enemy might assassinate (or execute) her husband for his taunting defense of his religious convictions.

So she worried. She worried about making ends meet, considering her husband's less-than-stable income and his fiscal carelessness. She worried about his safety; he was a marked man before she married him. She worried about his health—almost continual afflictions of one variety or another, some more serious than others. She must have also worried about her own health, considering her near-death experience at the time of her last pregnancy and miscarriage. She worried about the children, and with good reason, ever mindful of the terrible loss of her two daughters, baby Elizabeth and teenager Magdalena. And she worried about the kids' lifestyles and habits. And after her husband's death, her worries multiplied. She was a worrywart.

Luther had a ready solution for her worries: he admonished her to read his small catechism, as well as John's gospel, chiding her for her choosing to worry and treating God as though he were not "almighty."

Apparently imagining he could impress her with God's almightiness and calm her nerves, he assured her that God "could create ten Doctor Martins in case the old one should drown in the Saale"[6]—as though she'd want ten Martins. One was indeed enough.

Why spend energy worrying about his poor health and her inability to care for him so far away? He has someone who is far superior to her, as his letter from Eisleben had made clear: "I have a caretaker who is better than you and all the angels . . . who sits even so at the right hand of God the Father Almighty." And he adds: "Therefore, be content."[7] Or, as an earlier translator worded Luther's command, "Tranquillize thyself, then."[8]

Essentially, his message is, "Just buck up and be content, Katie." And if that doesn't work, he tells her he would comfort her in person— were he able to get out of his sick bed and come home to her. Knowing her worries, he consoled her by saying how tenderly he would love her if he were there with her.[9]

How little times have changed since the sixteenth century when it comes to giving advice to those who worry—except that back then, Katie could not Google her worries away. Simple enough for the twenty-first-century Christian. Enter the words *christians and worry*. I found numerous websites displayed from top to bottom on the menu screen.[10]

John MacArthur, on his *Grace to You* website, emphasizes sin over consolation: "We all have to admit that worry is a common temptation in life—for many it is a favorite pastime." Really? For Katie (and for me too), it would not be our idea of fun. But he goes on. Like certain other pastimes, "worry is a sin. It is neither insignificant, nor inconsequential. And for the Christian, it is absolutely contrary to faith in Christ." MacArthur's next four words makes any kind of consolation seem out of place: "Jesus categorically prohibited worry."[11] So there, Katie.

As we move down the menu, David Peach offers "7 Tips for Christians" in his top-titled article "How to Stop Worrying: 7 Tips for Christians." (1.2K people *Like* his tips.) We have no reason to assume Katie would have *Liked* his tips any more than she liked her husband's tips. But perhaps Katie would appreciate the next item on the menu, Jill Briscoe's testimony—"Why Can't I Stop Worrying?"

> I am a worrier. Yes, I know. I'm a Christian and Christians aren't supposed to worry. To give you an idea of how long this has been going on, our eldest son's first words were, "Oh dear!" That was well over 40 years ago. I'd been a Christian worker for many years when he said that, and I was a missionary to boot![12]

As we scroll further down the menu, *Christianity Today* weighs in with an essay by the editors titled "How Can I Overcome My Tendency to Worry?" Next is *Today's Christian Women*, with five strategies for "winning over worry" by Ginger Kolbaba. And then there is Joyce Meyer, "The Cause and Cure for Worry," an article found on her own website.

At this point, it is not difficult to imagine that Katie, looking at her computer screen amid all her worries, would just say, *I've got work to do*.

She truly did have work to do, and if there is any common denominator in her various duties, it was to protect her family—those who were nearest and dearest to her. Her husband's health was not good. As early as Martin's stay at the Wartburg Castle, he had complained of an assortment of ailments, and as he grew older, chronic disorders were simply part of his life.

And if health concerns were not enough to create distractions, the hopeful political and religious gains had gone in reverse or reared up and galloped headlong into danger. To see her husband distressed over his legacy and threatened on every side by enemies caused Katie many worrisome days and nights. Martin also feared for the Reformation's staying power, and he was well aware of his own health limitations. He had written as much to Katie on a number of occasions when he was felled by illness while out of town. Their very tight marriage partnership did not allow him to keep secrets, even regarding his own health. Yet he knew it would only make her worry even more.

Indeed, the political situation was threatening their very way of life in Wittenberg. In the summer of 1545, little more than six months before he died, Luther wrote to Katie of his despair. She understood. He had few friends left, and he emphasized that he wished to move elsewhere without even returning home. The great Reformer was *persona non grata* in his own hometown.[13]

Then he asked her to dispose of much of which she had put her whole heart into: "I would like you to sell garden, land, house, and courtyard; and then I shall restore the large house to my most gracious lord."[14] Luther knows his days are numbered, and this is in preparation for Katie's widowhood. Concerned about his own longevity, he wrote that he was hopeful that his prince benefactor would continue to support him as long as he lived.[15]

The future is very uncertain regarding money matters. Martin is hopeful but is also concerned about his salary, whether there will be adequate pension for Katie: "For I trust my most gracious lord would continue my salary for at least one year of my closing life." He knows how much she is worrying, and he's worried as well. Aware of his own enemies in Wittenberg, he was even more concerned about those who would not tolerate her after he died, which he feared would be soon. He desired that she get things in order before that time—especially to get out of "this Sodom" of Wittenberg.[16]

Imagine Katie reading such a letter from a man who tells her not to worry—to let God do the worrying. He knows he is dying; he adores her; he wants to make the transition to widowhood as smooth as it could possibly be considering the circumstances. If only she had the confidence in God that he had. How he must have stormed heaven on her behalf. He knew it was not enough to badger her to be a good Christian.

Besides quoting Scripture to her, however, Martin had other means of trying to calm Katie's nerves, the most obvious being humor. We want to think he could hear her voice through the distance and feel the vibrations of her hearty laugh. Why else would he have written the comical letter of February 10, 1546, now only eight days before his death:

To the saintly worrying Lord Katherine . . .

We thank you heartily for being so worried that you can't sleep, for since you started worrying about us, a fire broke out near my door and yesterday, no doubt due to your worry, a big stone, save for the dear angels, would have fallen and crushed us like a mouse in a trap. If you don't stop worrying, I'm afraid the earth will swallow us. Haven't you learned the Catechism and don't you believe? Pray and let God worry. "Cast your burden on the Lord." We are well except that Jonas banged his ankle. He is jealous of me and wanted to have something the matter with him, too. We hope soon to be released from this assignment and come home.[17]

Here amid his droll humor, he slips in Scripture and the hope they will be reunited soon, while not denying his serious illness. In many ways, it is Luther at his best.

Everyday worries like Katie's are the very concerns of our own day. I'm old enough to remember back in the 1970s when interest rates on savings accounts ranged between 15 and 20 percent. That sounds great, except for the fact that inflation was running wild. It's easy to imagine that such money matters are unique to modern life. But in a letter to Catharine Jonas in the spring of 1542, Luther had written, "Everything is going well here [in Wittenberg] except that the treasury and taxation has run wild. Otherwise, living is so cheap as never before, a sack of corn for three groats."[18] We understand why taxation would be a worry to Katie the landowner, but why should cheap living be a cause for concern? It is easy to forget she was at times a producer as well as a consumer—a seller of sacks of corn as well as a buyer.

Luther continues in this letter to Catharine with information we would consider very private today—and perhaps what Katie would have considered private back then. After his usual reference to her—"my Katie, now lord of Zülsdorf, greets you kindly"—he divulges details of her financial portfolio: "She lets herself be rated at nine thousand gulden, including the Black Cloister." Who knew women had credit scores back in the sixteenth century? And why would the husband disclose in a letter the details of such personal information? Was he too proud of her to keep silent—a woman to whom he had bragging rights? Ever thinking about his own demise, he qualifies her financial security by adding, "She will not have an annual income of one hundred gulden from the property after my death. But my gracious lord [the Elector] has kindly given more than I asked."[19]

Katie worried about how she would support herself after Martin's death. He, if not being worried, did show concern for the matter—even though they were well-to-do by standards of the day. But just as it is today, those with financial portfolios worry more than those who have no investments to worry about.

If we were to sum up Katie's worries, we could take a line from one of Martin's friends: she was "the partner of his calamities."[20] Luther's calamities came in many forms, and Katie was his wife, his partner. But was she really a partner in his great religious calamities? At times he sought to make her so. In fact, in 1540, he claimed that she was the one who convinced him to write against Erasmus. But Luther did not just take to task his religious adversaries' beliefs and writings. He viciously attacked them personally. He likened Erasmus to Judas Iscariot and implied he was no more than an atheist. "I vehemently and from the very heart hate Erasmus," he seethed, and the very mention of his name at table "sent Luther into a paroxysm of loathing."[21]

But why Erasmus, who had himself strongly criticized the church? Why Erasmus, a man who "loved peace," who was a "scholar and critic, more fitted for the study than for the crowd"?[22] Did Katie incite him? That would be a claim that is hard to swallow. Richard Marius goes on to assess the two men: "The temperaments of the two men were radically different." And what might have troubled—and worried—Katie on many occasions was how lethal her husband's anger often was, as Marius points out: "The intensity of this hatred [for Erasmus] is striking, even in Luther, for whom hatreds seemed as common as rocks in a quarry."[23]

How often the worrywart Katie must have wished her husband would settle down and not throw so many needlessly provocative rocks. The figurative rocks were hurled back at him, but did she fear the day was coming when rock throwing and attacks against him would be far more than figurative? And how did she feel when sitting at table when his personality turned into a paroxysm of loathing, a pathological convulsion of rage? She was wise enough to know that such rage affected not only his reputation but also his physical health. Trying to change his inner fury and frenzied demeanor would have been beyond her capability. So she worried—as any loving wife would have.

Did she wonder if he would go over the edge, not only in his angry outbursts, but also in his attacks of dark despair—his black dog? It happens—then and now. As I write, I'm reminded of a prominent minister in my own denomination, who for a lengthy period of time was the pastor of a church only blocks from my home. He was active at the yearly synod meetings, eager to engage with any controversial issue, confidently striding across the stage to the microphone to make his articulate and sharply worded case. He was hardly a Martin Luther, but one who surely did not shy away from the public forum and was thoroughly capable of holding his own in any argument. Did his wife worry about him? She knew things no observer from afar or even his closest colleagues would have known. After he retired from full-time ministry, he and his wife moved away. Shortly afterward, it became public knowledge (after he had gone missing) that he had only days before been released from a health facility due to depression. When his body was found more than a year later, empty pill bottles were close by.

What a tragedy! Christian psychobabble tells us that worry is sin, that depression is sin—and thus it's typically hidden from those who would use it to discredit another. One of Martin Luther's good attributes is that he did not cover up his dark depression, though he was seriously afflicted throughout his life. He suffered from severe and often acute depression (manifested by intense sweating), and by 1527, according to Richard Marius, he "was already showing symptoms of the heart disease that eventually killed him. He had chest pains, dizzy spells, and indigestion and sometimes fainted."[24] He was considerably overweight, despite Katie's pleading for him to watch his diet.

What was going on in his "tortured mind"?[25] The dark depression had manifested itself in the summer of 1527, as he wrote in a letter to Philip Melanchthon: "I almost completely lost Christ and I was plunged into the waves and tempests of desperation and blasphemy against God."[26] The depression continued to erupt in 1528, 1529, and beyond. "When we survey Luther's illnesses after 1527," writes Martin Brecht, "it is obvious that in the meantime he had become an unstable man."[27]

If only Katie had written down her own feelings and assessment, and if only they had been saved for posterity. Surely she was at times beside herself with worry. Unlike his down-to-earth, practical wife, Luther regarded physical problems in spiritual terms and believed the best response was prayer.[28] But Katie's very practical mind-set must have desperately wished there were an herb—or a modern-day pill—to calm his nerves. Yet, "for a man whose habits were manifestly unhealthful, he lived to a remarkable age, dying in his sixty-third year."[29]

"Luther was to make more of Satan as the years went along," writes Richard Marius. This was true in his early years, "but the preoccupation with Satan seems not to have been so intense, so personal" then. "In time Satan became for Luther a personalized expression of the powers of darkness, a brother to death."[30] Indeed, "Luther appears to have been hypersensitive to death's terrors . . . For whatever reason, he was unable to build up the wall of denial that allows most of us to lead relatively 'healthy-minded' lives."[31]

Katie and his friends were fully aware, she having observed his terrors in person. In fact, he would turn to her in the middle of the night while he was stricken and beg her, "Forbid me to have such temptations."[32] Had she not seen the chilling effects of such night terrors (daytime as well), we might picture her rolling over with a dismissive, "Whatever." But she knew how serious his despair was and how significantly his physical health was affected. How long did she lie awake worrying?

When we seek to assess the psychological and spiritual differences between Katie and Martin, we see that he is what many regard as a spiritual giant. But emotionally he seems to have been significantly weaker than she. Her spirituality was pragmatic. She truly was a worrywart, but often with good reason. If someone wishes to hold that against her and point out this *sin*, she would ignore the slight and go about her hectic schedule. She worried as she worked, all the while turning her worry into strategies to keep her family financially afloat and alive and well.

What Katie did not need was her husband or any self-appointed critics ordering her not to worry or telling her that worrying is sin and to just stop sinning. What she did need was her husband's assurance of love and good humor. And we hope she sometimes sensed the soft-spoken counsel of Jesus. Perhaps she had moments to pause and hear his words of consolation:

> Do not worry, dear Katie, about how you're going to feed forty hungry mouths or brew enough beer for all those who come to table, how you're going to finish mending or washing all those piles of laundry, or even how you're going to keep that fragile and overwrought husband of yours from going over the edge. Take a little time out for yourself; try not to worry about the morrow, for you know that each day has enough trouble of its own. Slow down and smell the lilies of the field. They toil not and neither do they spin, and just look at them blowing so easily in the breeze. Come unto me, dear Katie, you who labor and are so heavy laden. I will give you rest.[33]

"Fifty Gulden" Bible Reading

UNDERVALUED SPIRITUALITY

er piety is more a matter of inference than record,"[1] observed Preserved Smith. Does Katie come up short on piety—on the spiritual side of life? That is one of the questions we explore in this chapter.

How do we judge an individual's spirituality, especially if we are looking for a role model? A Mother Teresa who devotes her life to serving the poorest of the poor? A megachurch minister who has his own TV program and writes bestselling books? A pope who forsakes red Prada shoes and washes the feet of homeless derelicts? Only God knows the heart. But we all make judgments.

So how do we even begin to comprehend Katharina's spiritual life—and even that of her husband? Martin has been judged harshly in reference to his vulgarities and anti-Semitism. Yet he had a profound spiritual nature that was invigorated by his love for theological and biblical scholarship. His letter writing and words at table are filled with godly counsel and pious platitudes. And what of Katie? Neither of them, we can conclude, warrant canonization as a saint, even if Protestants had carried on the tradition.

As I pondered how one might assess Katie's spirituality, I have called forth dozens of women from the pages of Scripture as well as from Christian history. As a hardworking wife and businesswoman, Katie's biblical match was the Proverbs 31 woman. And actually, like Katie, this woman in Proverbs is not a model for our typical ideal of true spirituality. "She certainly is a remarkable woman," writes Rich Deem. "However, I maintain she is *not* the ideal *Christian* wife . . . What do we know about [her] prayer life? Nothing! We don't know if she *ever* prayed." Deem goes on to observe that this woman was like Martha in the Gospels, "a typical type A personality" who "got irked that her sister [Mary] was sitting" listening to Jesus instead of helping her prepare the meal.[2]

Mary, the sister of Martha, as we so easily assess her spirituality, is not a biblical match for Katie. But I wonder if Mary, the mother of Jesus, might be. Even suggesting her name, however, is nothing short of shocking. After all, she is the most adored saint of the Catholic Church. How could a runaway nun stand spiritually alongside her? Such a comparison requires us to recognize Mary for who she was—a down-to-earth first-century Palestinian woman.

In Luke's gospel, we learn that Gabriel appeared and told her that she had been chosen to give birth to the Messiah. Whether or not she recognized this mighty angel, the experience was terrifying. But she has the wherewithal to question the news. She knows better—virgins don't have babies. Gabriel explains. She solemnly accepts the commission. But only after her cousin Elizabeth blesses her does she sing the Magnificat. And what a song it is. So far there is little comparison between Mary and Katie, except that we glimpse Mary as a confident and questioning woman in her own right. When we meet the virgin Katie as a young adult, she also would have sung that same Magnificat at the Cistercian monastery of Marienthron (Mary's throne).

"Mary's story is that of an ordinary woman," writes Scot McKnight. "Mary has become for many little more than a compliant 'resting womb' for God, and she has become a stereotype of passivity in the face of challenge . . . quietude to the point of hiding in the shadows of others."[3]

Truly the biblical Mary was an ordinary woman. Argula von

Grumbach and others argued that in the sixteenth century. There is no evidence she was both sinless and a virgin her entire life. The Gospels make clear that Mary had children after she gave birth to Jesus, both sons and daughters. In fact, like Katie, she probably had at least six children. And Joseph, like Martin, was apparently much older than his wife. Soon after Mary sings the Magnificat, and after Katie leaves the convent, both are focused on child rearing. If Mary spent much of her life praying (as the concrete statues suggest), the Gospels make no direct reference to it.

In her book *God's Ideal Woman*, Dorothy Pape challenges Bible expositors who have characterized Mary as a behind-the-scenes homebody. "But with the possible exception of the angel's announcement of the coming conception," writes Pape, "the scriptural record never shows us Mary at home." Katie spent much of her time at her Black Cloister boardinghouse, but like Mary she was often on the road: Mary "is hurrying off to Elizabeth," Pape continues, "then going to Bethlehem for the census, then to Jerusalem for purification rites, down to Egypt, back to Nazareth, then to Jerusalem again for the Passover, to Cana for the wedding, to Capernaum, to a city near the Sea of Galilee with her other sons to persuade Jesus to come home, and finally to Jerusalem again."[4]

And we can imagine Mary bustling around Nazareth, much like Katie did in Wittenberg. In fact, there is a statue of Katie in Wittenberg that shows her not in prayer but walking, almost on the run. It would be fitting if statues of Mary depicted her in the same way.

Both women present fascinating accounts of spiritual uncertainties. Mary is not fully aware of the implications of the gospel and her son's role in it. She frets when she discovers that her boy is not with the returning Passover crowds, and she appears more than a little irritated when she learns he had purposely stayed behind to talk to learned men in the temple: "Son, why have you treated us like this," she demands. "Your father and I have been anxiously searching for you" (Luke 2:48). Years later, when religious leaders were condemning Jesus and saying he was possessed by Beelzebul, his mother and brothers "went to take charge of him, for they said, 'He is out of his mind'" (Mark 3:21). Mary fears for her son's sanity and wants to bring him home. Another version is even stronger: "they went out to take custody of Him; for they were saying, 'He has lost His senses'" (Mark 3:21 NASB).

Katie in a similar way feared for her husband—that he might lose his senses. And she was sometimes less than certain about the implications of the Reformation. Obviously, the two women played very different roles in salvation history, and Mary's place is truly on display in biblical proportions. But in the Gospels, she emerges as a very normal first-century woman. It seems unfortunate that we so easily imagine her as an untouchable saint, the gold standard of spirituality. Katie is not seen as such a model, but she too is often airbrushed as a saintly heroine. How important it is to let both women be themselves.

As already noted, viewing Katie alongside Martha in the Gospels, rather than her sister Mary, is not a stretch. "Without marked spirituality," writes Preserved Smith, Katie "was a Martha busied with many things rather than a Mary [Martha's sister] sitting in devotion at her master's feet."[5] Like the Proverbs 31 woman, and for that matter, most of the women in the Hebrew Bible, Katie is not on record as being unusually devout.

Although there are stories of how Martin rose early in the morning to pray, no one has ever suggested that Katie got up at 4:30 for devotions. She rose before dawn to begin her workday. We might wonder if she had gotten all prayed out when she was in the convent. In fact, if we were to characterize Katie's spirituality after 1525, we would see it most plainly realized in marriage, motherhood, and hard work.

In that sense, she was very different from her God-intoxicated husband. "He makes most sense," writes Martin Marty, "as a wrestler with God, indeed, as a God-obsessed seeker of certainty and assurance in a time of social trauma and of personal anxiety."[6]

One of the stories sometimes told about Katie relates to her challenging not only the Bible but also her husband. As the account goes,

Martin was reading about God commanding Abraham to sacrifice his son Isaac (Genesis 22). Katie was adamant that God would never command a father to kill his own child. Martin, of course, corrected her and said that's exactly what God did.[7] Whether Katie pressed her point or let it go is not recorded, but the story demonstrates how differently the two of them perceived God, and it also demonstrates Katie's ease in challenging her husband's claims on Scripture. And maybe the story has something to say about gender. I've known women in my own circle of acquaintances who have strongly objected to an account of Abraham acquiescing without argument—Abraham, the very man who bargained boldly with God in an effort to save Sodom.

Katie, as we have come to know her, was more emotionally balanced than her erratic husband. He struggled with black depression and spiritual despair. "He was sure" writes Marty, "that the nagging, even horrifying *Anfechtungen* that assaulted him as a young professor and then lifelong were a plague to everyone . . . *Anfechtungen* attacked with a voice that came during what he called the night battles in the dark chambers of the cloister and of his soul." Though difficult to define, this was an "inner voice . . . that haunted him," questioning the very "existence or reality of God." Luther was convinced that those "who wanted and needed to find and be found right with a gracious God must struggle."[8]

Everyone? There is no evidence at all that Katie ever wrestled with God, and certainly not in such dramatic ways as did her husband. She was a woman of the world who had to manage a vast household and farm. There was no time to wrestle with God, especially when she was forced to wrestle with a husband battling demons and the darkness within his own soul.

As stated earlier, the story is also told how Katie confronted Martin on one occasion after he had fallen into a deep, black depression. She took her mourning dress out of storage, put it on, and confronted him in the hallway. "Who died?" the professor asked. "God," she told him. "You foolish thing," said Martin. "Why this foolishness?" She was ready with an answer: "It is true. God must have died, or Doctor Luther would not be so mournful."[9] He considered her words. Indeed, he *was* behaving as though God were dead. Some have cited this story as evidence of Katie's spiritual insight, but it is more properly seen as a simple object lesson that she hoped would help pull her husband out of his depression.

We should not imagine that most women of the sixteenth century who identified with the Reformation were like Katie—more Martha than Mary—in their spirituality. A number of women wanted to get in on the action: writing treatises, tracts, testimonies, and in other ways defending the tenets of Reformed beliefs, not the least of whom were Argula von Grumbach and Katherine Zell. And they both strongly defended their spiritual heritage by speaking out.

Argula's heroes were Deborah and Esther, while at the same time she was concerned about what she perceived as biblical constraints. "I am not unacquainted with the word of Paul that women should be silent in church," she conceded, "but, when no man will or can speak, I am driven by the word of the Lord when he said 'He who confesses me on earth, him will I confess and he who denies me, him will I deny.'"[10] She was willing to break the law by conducting religious meetings at her home and officiating at funerals. She faithfully carried on Luther's reform, outliving him by nearly two decades. The "old Staufferin," as the Duke of Bavaria cynically describes her, was twice imprisoned, the last time at age seventy shortly before her death. She, not Katie, stands as a spiritual role model.

Katherine Zell likewise defended her preaching by citing biblical precedent. But Katie had no reason to defend herself with Scripture. It is, however, tempting to put words in her mouth—words that help convince the reader that she was a pious evangelical, a role model who demonstrates how we ought to live. Hollie Dermer's writing illustrates this as she prays a prayer for Katie—a prayer spoken more to her readers than to God:

Once Katie found out that they were indeed to be wed she reflected and then prayed:

> *"Now I shall no longer be Katharina, runaway nun;*
> *I shall be the wife of the great Doctor Luther, and everything*
> *I do or say will reflect upon him . . . It's like an assignment*
> *from God. God, keep me humble. Help me to be a good wife*
> *to your servant Doctor Luther. And perhaps, dear Father,*
> *You can also manage to give me a little love and happiness."*

God heard and answered Katie's prayer. The Lord blessed them with a very loving, caring marriage.[11]

We long for Katie's actual words, though not these. "There are no records to give insights into how Katharina herself discerned her religious calling," writes Kirsi Stjerna,[12] who deals with Katie's life from her convent years through her two decades as a minister's wife. But whether a calling or not, she made a profound vocational decision in "facing the unknown and leaving what was for all practical purposes her only family," her sisters at the convent.[13] And what can we make of her spiritual life during the several years she was a nun, as well as during the two years after she escaped? Considering Luther's condemnation of monasticism, it would be of interest to know her assessment of the system. It is striking that there is no evidence that Katie looked back at her life at the convent in negative terms. Other nuns escaped and brought with them tales of misery and despair. She would have had the perfect forum at the table, but none of the students or other guests ever reported such comments from her. Nor did her husband recount any claims of abuse or unhappiness. Unlike Florentina von Oberweimar, who told a disparaging story of convent life (published in a tract with an endorsement by Martin Luther himself), Katie may have been relatively content and not an active participant in the conspiratorial plans to escape.[14]

At one point, Katie asked her husband, "Why is it that under the pope we prayed so ardently and frequently and that now our prayers are so cold and rare?" His response, interestingly, seems to speak for them both: "We were [then] driven that way [but now] we are so ice cold and lazy in our prayers that we are not consistent in them."[15] We wonder if Luther was chiding Katie more than himself with "ice cold and lazy." We know from other sources and his own writings that the phrase would not describe his own outlook—unless he was in the midst of despair. Katie's own words—"cold and rare"—are telling.

Katie's praying "ardently and frequently" at the convent also says volumes. Not all nuns could thus speak. Convents were typically not left to their own devices, and that was true of Marienthron. A supervising abbot was assigned to check up on the nuns, and he visited the convent regularly. He was not at all impressed by the devotional life of the nuns, regarding them as slackers in their observance of prayer and careless in their times of collective worship.[16] Was Katie one of those lax in worship? Or did she pray, as Martin suggested, only because she was driven to do so? Or did she pray "feverishly, diligently, and frequently,"[17] from the heart, as she later recalled. She hardly appears to be driven.

Whether Katie first entered and then left the convent for spiritual reasons—reasons bolstered by Martin's biblical and theological arguments—is certainly not clear from the available sources. Indeed, there is no evidence that Luther, in all his complimentary comments about her both in letters and at table, ever spoke of her as being an exemplary convert to his teachings, as, for example, Argula was. Whether or not Katie truly thought through his teachings before she escaped, the longing for freedom no doubt was a powerful motivation in itself.

Most of the German nuns in this era did not enter a religious life with unbounded enthusiasm. In fact, many resented the restrictions, and not just those who became enflamed by Reformation teachings. The abbess Verena von Stuben and her nuns at the well-endowed convent of Sonnenburg illustrate this. When Cardinal Nicholas of Cusa (appointed in 1452) sought to institute monastic reform in all the territories of Germany, she balked, as did other well-heeled noble-women. She had work to do administering her lands and attending politically important weddings, and she could not do it all herself. The nuns willingly ran errands to the village and far beyond.

That she should be cloistered was absurd. Besides (no doubt rolling her eyes at the thought), Cusa was merely a "bourgeois Rhinelander."[18] Who was he to order her around? He did, however, have the power of the church behind him. So she eventually offered a compromise. Cusa could reform the nuns, but she would be exempt. Cusa was adamant. His expectations were clear. The abbess was to be far more than an administrator. Her first duty was to serve as a spiritual role model to the nuns, who would look up to her in their training and devotion to God. More specifically, she was to be present at most, if not all, of the daily hours, choirs, masses, and vespers, not gadding about outside the convent, involved in business or social engagements unbefitting to an abbess.[19]

When she refused to comply, Cusa ordered her out and appointed his own handpicked abbess. However, Verena managed to stay in control and stall the process for six years, but in the end, it was no contest. The Cardinal not only excommunicated her but also placed the convent under interdict, which among other things did not allow a priest to administer Mass—a huge deal even for flighty nuns. If that were not enough, he used his power to halt all rent payments and put an embargo on food and fuel deliveries. Even the mercenaries who delivered supplies at the behest of Verena's brother-in-law could not break Cusa's stranglehold, and Verena, this "true Jezebel,"[20] as Cusa called her, was forced to retire. Yet in the years that followed, she won significant victories, including a "handsome annual pension" and a lifting of the ban that had been placed on her and the convent. It is no doubt an understatement: "The cloister was never successfully reformed."[21]

What is most significant about this account is the drastic gap between expectations and reality—particularly in light of the church's efforts to reform the convents by tightening discipline. Such reform efforts were well underway when Katharina was progressing through the monastic system. What we wouldn't give to be a fly on the wall observing her and her compliance with spiritual expectations. Did she participate with passion, or did she merely go through the motions?

What if Katharina had become a celebrated abbess with all the spunk she demonstrated as a ruling matron of the Black Cloister? How different her life would have been—and dare we say, less fulfilling. Unlike some celebrated abbesses, Katie had no deep spiritual insights to offer. She was no Hildegard, who filled her days and notebooks with vivid revelations and messages from God. From what we know of Katie, such spirituality would not have easily conformed to her psychological makeup. What *did* conform was discussion at table, and she was not simply a silent observer.

On one occasion, she challenged her husband: "How could David say, 'Judge me according to my righteousness,' when he didn't have any?"[22] Good question. Hadn't her husband repeatedly quoted Paul that none of us have righteousness? Luther liked to brag about his wife, as in a letter he wrote in 1535. He sent greetings, as he often did, from not just "Katie," but "my *lord* Katie," boasting about her wide-ranging activities, including planning fields and selling cows. But the kicker in this letter was to say that he had baited her with a hefty amount of money—50 gulden—if she would finish reading the Bible before Easter, having already nearly read through the Pentateuch.[23] But the outcome was not assured. When he was nagging at her to reach the goal he had set, she reportedly sassed back, "I've read enough. I've heard enough. I know enough. Would to God I lived it."[24]

Katie's primary understanding of Scripture, we can assume, came not from reading but rather from her sitting at table as her husband interacted with students. Though it may have been a backhanded compliment, Luther on one occasion reportedly remarked, "Katie understands the Bible better than any papists did twenty years ago."[25]

Since he assumed that "papists" two decades removed understood next to nothing about the Bible, we might wish he would have offered a more convincing compliment. But there are indications she was biblically and theologically competent, if not astute. Indeed, we imagine her as wife, mother, and entrepreneur, not particularly a scholar. But she did enjoy sitting at table listening to the discussions and debates among students and her husband. From the "table talk" notes, it appears she was not always appreciated, but she was *Doctorissa*, perhaps only to designate that she was "Doctor" Luther's wife. We know from correspondence, as well as from "table talk," that she understood enough Latin to interact with matters being discussed.[26]

But the fact remains that Katie was more a Martha than a Mary who was focused on learning at the feet of Jesus. When Luther had been so ill in the summer of 1527 that he and some of his closest friends believed he was dying, he prepared for the end: "In a loud prayer he surrendered himself to God's will,"[27] as he had repeatedly done. But the assurance he needed most was not from God. "Several times he turned to his 'beloved Katy,' admonishing her to submit to God's will. She should remember that she, the former nun, was his wife and she should concentrate on God's Word."[28]

Dr. Katie was known for her medical skills, and she was on call when a serious problem arose and often exchanged helpful hints with other women in the community. In fact, at times the Black Cloister became a virtual hospital. Luther highly approved of this ministry to the sick, but he had concerns. Expertise and medicine were not enough. He wrote about this problem that "our wives, even Kate, experience: that intercession [to God] applies only to their husbands, not to them. Consequently, to the women's disadvantage, they do not use it [prayer and Scripture] when they need it."[29]

Katie would have no doubt responded that the women—particularly when confronting a serious medical issue like a difficult birth—were too focused on what had to be done. Let the men do the praying. He had written to her about prayer when he was away in 1540, urging her to pray, not for him specifically, but for another reason: "Pray diligently, as you owe it to our Lord Christ."[30]

Luther felt compelled to nag Katie to improve her devotional life. Not so Philip Melanchthon with regard to his wife Catherine, if the words of Joachim Camerarius are taken at face value:

> She was a very pious woman, who loved her husband devotedly; an industrious and active mother of her family, liberal and benevolent towards all, and so careful for the interests of the poor, that she did not only lose sight of her ability and strength in the distribution of her charities, but even interceded for them among her friends, with the greatest earnestness, and even impetuosity. She led a spotless life, and was so anxious to cultivate a pious and honorable character, that she did not concern herself about expensive entertainments, or costly dress.[31]

It is difficult to imagine Katie being described as "very pious" or leading a "spotless life . . . so anxious to cultivate a pious and honorable character." In many respects, this first lady of the Reformation, the one who is referred to as the first Protestant pastor's wife, was an ordinary woman of her times married to a man who led a far less than spotless life himself. Her pride and prejudices often mirrored his own, and we dare not clothe her (or him) with an undeserved mantle of Christian graciousness. Her apparent anti-Semitism is evident in a letter from Martin in 1545 (a year before his death), telling her how he suddenly became physically weak and dizzy as he and his party were approaching Eisleben. He tells her that his severe headache was [for whatever reason] his own fault. He goes on, however, to make a crude anti-Semitic joke, which he would have assumed Katie would find humorous, saying that if she had been with him, she would have blamed it on the Jews, who were blowing a cold, icy wind at him. If he were not so consumed with theological reform, he tells her, he would focus his attention on ridding the country of Jews.[32]

How did she react to that letter? We don't know. Did she laugh in agreement, or did she wish that her husband would behave more like a good Christian? Unfortunately, the way to understanding Katie is through her husband, and his letters and talk at table are often inconclusive.

Martin's words to Katie in his letters of February 1546, less than two weeks before he died, as previously noted, however, are quite revealing:

> Dear Kate, read *St. John* and the smaller *catechism*, of which you once said: Really everything in this book is applicable to me. For you want to care for your God, precisely as if he were not almighty, and could create ten *Dr. Martins*, if this aged one should perish in the Saale, or in the oven, or on Wolf's bird-decoy.[33]

Here Martin packs a lot in a very short paragraph: read the gospel of John and the smaller catechism, reminding her of her own words—that she had once said that *everything* in at least one of the books was applicable to her. What follows is more difficult to discern through translation. But he seems to be accusing her of wanting to care for her God as though he were *not* almighty. In some ways, that assessment sums up Katie's spirituality—and that of many of us. She went about her daily tasks guided by the axiom that "God helps those who help themselves." Martin, however, stressed prayer and God's almightiness in every aspect of life.

Unlike her husband, Katie did not have people hovering around her bedside, begging for final words and confessions, when she died. Indeed, the only final words we have from her come in dozens of versions in English alone, including, "I will cling to Jesus"; "I will cling to Christ like a burr on a dress [like a burr on a topcoat; like a burr to a frock]"; "I will stick to Christ like a burr on cloth"; "I cling to my Lord Christ"; and J. H. Alexander's version: "I will cling to Christ like a burr on a velvet coat."[34] What a holy way to depart this world of physical pain—except that such platitudes are untrue.

Like almost every effort to put pious words in Katie's mouth, this saying comes with dubious authenticity. "The quote has been popularly ascribed to Katharina Luther, née von Bora, as her deathbed expression of faith."[35] But despite its many recurrences and its attribution to her, it more properly belongs to Duchess Katharina of Saxony, and the words may very well have been put in her mouth as well. They were transferred to Katie in the nineteenth century.[36]

In one sense the burr analogy is fitting. Katie the farmer would have had many of them clinging to her skirt. Her spirituality was infused with hard work, often out in the fields. She would have hitched up her rough woolen skirt and would still have to yank off the annoying burrs. So also her life, as the adage is remembered: "How full of briars [or burrs] is this working-day world!"[37]

Martin Luther comforted himself in the face of death, even as he had in the deaths of his daughters. His words of consolation, whether quoted with any precision or not, are vintage Luther: "You will rise again, and shine like a star, yea, as the sun. I am joyful in spirit, but I am sorrowful in the flesh. We . . . should not lament as those who have no hope; we have dismissed a saint, yea, a living saint for heaven. O, that we could so die! Such a death I would willingly accept this very hour."[38]

His words are not Katie's. There is no indication that her worldview was so spiritually optimistic. Her life was filled with burrs, especially those unbearable burrs of her daughters' and her husband's deaths—and that terrible burr of her own death, which meant leaving behind motherless children.

CHAPTER

"No Words Can Express My Heartbreak"

WIDOWHOOD AND FINAL YEARS

O God, if Luther is dead, who will henceforth deliver the Holy Gospel to us with such clearness?"[1] This lament is the heart cry of the great artist Albrecht Dürer, who would himself never live to hear the actual pronouncement, *Luther is dead*. The artist's fears were expressed in 1521 after Luther's excommunication at the Diet of Worms. Luther, however, would live for another quarter century. Indeed, he would continue to hold forth as a formidable religious leader. During those years, he escaped death on numerous occasions, either at the hands of an enemy or his own maladies. Yet for many, even in 1546, the words *Luther is dead* were alarming. Both enemies and friends were stunned. What would become of his legacy? The news confirmed Katie's worst fears.

Biographers often divide the lives of their subjects into manageable segments, as has frequently been done with Martin Luther. With Katharina, the task is relatively simple. There are four major events in her life, each marking the beginning and end of two lengthy stages: (1) her entry into monastic life as a young child and her escape from it, and (2) her marriage to Luther and his death. Details of her five years prior to entering the convent are lost to us. Not so, her final years as

171

a widow. Here we find her active and in control. In fact, during her nearly seven-year widowhood, as devastating as this season of life was, we see her rising up and taking charge amid blinding sorrow. She is independent, strong, and competent, even as she was in marriage.

From references to her at this time, however, it would be easy to characterize Katie during these final years as an irritable, belligerent, and hardened widow. And in many ways she was. Her problem was that she had the mind-set of an independent twenty-first-century widow more than that of a dependent sixteenth-century one.

The story begins with her husband's death. Fortunately for biographers, he was a celebrity in his lifetime. Every detail of his life after 1517 was carefully recorded, particularly his death. Heiko Oberman sums up his final week:

> In the last days before his death Luther had been the cheerful man his friends knew and loved. He had successfully completed a difficult mission: a trip from Wittenberg to Eisleben [where he had been born and baptized] to mediate in a protracted quarrel . . . After two tough weeks of negotiation, the parties had narrowed their differences and a reconciliation had finally— though only temporarily—been achieved. So there was reason to be cheerful . . . although he was quite sure he had little time left: "When I get home to Wittenberg again, I will lie down in my coffin and give the worms a fat doctor to feast on." By highlighting the skeleton within the human body, late medieval art had urgently reminded everyone that health, beauty, and wealth were only a few breaths away from the Dance of Death. The "fat doctor" was well aware of this, not as a moralistic horror story, but as a reality of life poised on the brink of eternity.[2]

This "Dance of Death" would have been very real to Katie in this era when bereavement was lurking somewhere beneath every rooftop in Wittenberg. But the suddenness of losing her husband was a searing pain. How does one cope with the loss of a beloved spouse? For me, the term *widowhood* spells fear, dread, and the indescribable sadness of losing my husband. He has visited that realm twice. For him, the terminal diagnoses (ovarian and pancreatic cancers) wrapped their shrouds around each marriage for more than three years, while family fun and laughter punched holes through the blackness. In the end, death turned into a painfully sad gift—no more chemo and unbearable physical suffering.

Although Martin had suffered painful afflictions, he was not terminally ill, and Katie would not have regarded his passing in any sense a gift. Amid her deep grief, however, she had no choice but to move on in all her work-related endeavors, confronting gender discrimination at every turn. Her rights over her estate and young children were far less than secure. When Martin died on February 18, 1546, there were four surviving children. Hans, nineteen, was by no means independent. Martin was fourteen; Paul had just turned thirteen; and Margarete was not yet eleven. And though Luther had thought he might die on several earlier occasions and had sought to prepare Katie for his death, there was not enough warning for her to even travel to be at his bedside.

Truly his death came with a suddenness that must have stunned her. He had previously been very ill, and his letters during earlier travels had shaken her to the core. But now, as his last letter to her clearly indicated, all was well. In fact, this final letter to her, written four days before he died, was among his most optimistic: "We can come home this week," he began—and very welcome news it was. "The dukes have made up. I'm going to invite them as guests that they may talk to each other."[3]

Why does he always do this to me? she might have been thinking. *And dukes? How am I supposed to properly house and feed them? Doesn't he know I can't handle any more freeloaders?*

Luther must have known she wouldn't be thrilled with more guests, and his next sentences would have pleased her: "I am sending you some trout which the Duchess of Hohenstein sent me. She is very happy over the reconciliation." The best news, besides his imminent homecoming, settled her mind on family matters: "The boys are still at Mansfeld. We are so well treated here that we are in danger of forgetting Wittenberg. The bladder stone, praise God, is not bothering me."[4]

How fitting it would have been if he had returned and she could have had some private parting words with him. She so desperately needed consolation, and there was no one who could have soothed her more than this German barbarian with whom she had lived for twenty years. Theirs was a solid marriage that never knew heart-pounding romance, but their partnership of deep and abiding affection carried them through joys and sorrows and hardships. Now this, the ultimate hardship. When the news arrived, the Black Cloister was never blacker.

But in fact, she was not the one to first officially hear the news: "Shortly after Doctor Martinus died at about 3:00 a.m. on February 18," writes Heiko Oberman, "Justus Jonas carefully recorded Luther's last twenty-four hours, addressing his report not to Luther's widow, as one might expect, but to his sovereign, Elector John Frederick, with a copy for his university colleagues in Wittenberg."[5]

It was important to have the death witnessed and recorded. Jonas had drawn up the letter in the predawn hours, less than two hours after Luther died. Besides Jonas, the witnesses included sons Martin and Paul, the court preacher, a servant, a notary and his wife, the inn owner, and two doctors. Children, friends, strangers—all but Katie. Another stranger, a doctor, "ascribed the death to a stroke of paralysis, brought on by the closing up of a wound in his leg from which the Reformer had suffered for years."[6]

Dressed in a white smock, Luther's corpse remained on the bed where he died until his death mask and coffin were prepared. Then the following afternoon, his body was taken to a nearby church, where Jonas preached a funeral sermon. The next day, after Katie had been informed by Philip Melanchthon, the funeral procession headed toward Wittenberg. As the parade passed through towns along the way, church bells pealed. Not until the morning of February 22, four days and a few hours after Martin died, did the procession arrive in Wittenberg at Elster Gate.

Heading the procession were various court representatives from Saxony, accompanied by dozens of mounted horsemen. It was a state funeral, with all the solemnity that would accompany the death of a prince or king. Katie and daughter Margarete had been driven out to meet the procession, and her wagon followed behind the hearse with the coffin draped in black. The three sons walked with other close relatives. Following them were professors, students, and town officials bringing up the rear. Johannes Bugenhagen gave the funeral oration, followed by personal reflections from Philip Melanchthon, "who did not make a secret of the fact that Luther was not a 'saint,' but a normal person who also had rough edges."[7] His place of burial was the famous Castle Church.

Melanchthon had written to Chancellor Brück about Katie's reaction to the news: "It is easy to see that the poor woman is deeply shocked and greatly troubled, but especially on account of the three sons whom the sainted Doctor had in Eisleben, not knowing how they might react to their father's death."[8]

How difficult it must have been for Katie to grieve privately for her husband, who belonged to all of Wittenberg and regions far beyond. Where could she go for consolation? She had very few friends, some of whom had predeceased her. Nor did she possess her husband's calm certainty that death meant moving on to a far better heavenly home. The finality of the deaths of her two daughters years earlier and now the death of her husband left her crushed.

For nearly three decades, Luther had been an important public figure, and his death was not a private matter related primarily to wife and family. His passing marked the end of an era. When Philip Melanchthon, while in the middle of a lecture at the university, was first given the news, he was crestfallen. His words needed no explanation: "The charioteer of Israel has fallen."[9] Others had already picked up the mantle, but the father of the Reformation, that sickly and rumpled prophet, had been, at least figuratively, transported to heaven in a chariot of fire.

Unlike Elijah, however, Martin Luther's final hours had been very carefully written for posterity. In fact, it would not be long before his enemies (as his followers feared) began spreading rumors that he had recanted on his deathbed or that he had undergone a miserable death at the hands of the devil or that he was guilty of the most unpardonable sin of suicide. And such rumors continue even today. On a website devoted to Luther, a man named Ray commented, "Growing up in a strict Catholic family, my dad would tell me stories of how Luther was racked by pain in his final moments, crying out to God to forgive him of the sins he committed against His Church, those present looking in horror as he screamed out that the demons were dragging him away."[10]

Katie was certainly used to such denunciations from her husband's opponents, but now she would have to face them alone. Worse, however, must have been the censure aimed directly at her. And she would realize that she had few friends. Even close relatives seemed almost aloof. When her sister-in-law Christina von Bora wrote to her requesting financial help for her son Florian, Katie, as her letter indicates, responded by emphasizing her present sorrow and brokenness:

> I see that you have a heartfelt sympathy for me and my poor children. For who should not properly be sad and worried on account of such a dear man as was my beloved husband . . . I can neither eat nor drink. And in addition to that, I cannot sleep. And if I had a principality or an empire I wouldn't feel so bad about losing it as I feel now that our dear Lord God has taken this beloved and dear man from me and not only from me, but from the whole world. When I think about it, I can't refrain from grief and crying either to read or to write, as God well knows.[11]

Doesn't it seem inappropriate that Katie was being hit on for funds only two months after her husband had been buried? But she could not simply let the matter drop. In her reply, she declined to take on the support of Florian's education. She implied that she was very poor, though in fact she was not. She "overstated the effect of her loss," writes Scott Hendrix. When taking into account "Luther's estate and the generosity of Elector John Frederick, the counts of Mansfield, and Luther's close colleagues, there was plenty of money."[12] In fact, at the time of his death, they would have been among the most affluent residents of Wittenberg. But Katie, the realist, knew how quickly a financial estate could turn to dust during these dark days of war and pestilence—and court orders.

"When Luther died," writes Erwin Weber, "Katharine's world fell apart." Although her husband had willed everything to her, and the Elector supported Luther's wishes, "the judges in the territory would not permit widows to inherit the estate and ordered guardians for her children."[13] Her future was unsettled, and she regarded it her responsibility alone to make sure she would be able to carry on. She could not depend on the men around her.

Her greatest concern was for the financial well-being of her children. Katie was first and foremost a mother hen, fearful of letting the chicks stray very far beyond her protective wings. When she had been away on business, she expected Martin to be the reliable househusband. But now there were those who were accusing her of seeking to amass a fortune for herself with no regard for her children. Thus, despite her husband's clear instructions in his will, she and the children were to have guardians. Her independence—and her very motherhood—was to be taken over by others. Only Margarete would live with her.

It's hard to imagine a committee deciding the fate of this fatherless family when the mother herself was fully competent to take over. But that is exactly what was happening. The Elector, his chancellor, Gregory Brück, and others met behind closed doors and made decisions that would then be conveyed to Katie. He was certainly no friend of Katie, accusing her of caring less for her children than for enriching herself. He vowed he would ruin her by sending her children away and putting an end to what he insisted was her profligate spending. He paid no heed to Martin's clear instructions that his capable wife, Katie, be their children's guardian.[14]

But Martin Luther was dead, and now was the time to put Katie in her place. Brück's decisions were driven by spitefulness. "At any rate, in his aversion toward Katie and in his wish to sever her influence," writes Ernst Kroker, "he now became unfair toward her. He cast suspicion on her with the Elector . . . Even less should he have implied that he twice came upon the rumor that Katie might get married again."[15]

Property was also a major matter of conflict. Katie and Martin had often disagreed on the acquisition of property, but her wishes had prevailed. Now after his death, she believed her only financial security lay in more land. He feared taking such risks amid political and military uncertainties.[16] Who would work the land? There would be taxes to pay with no income. But Katie was determined to purchase more. "Against the advice of former chancellor Brück and Melanchthon," writes Scott Hendrix, "Katharina purchased a low-lying farm at Wachsdorf."[17] It was a two-hour journey from Wittenberg, but not as far away as her Zülsdorf farm.

Why couldn't Katie simply take the advice of others, especially Chancellor Brück? Why not make life easier—"send all the boys to school, dispose of the property, return the Black Cloister to the Elector, and live with her daughter modestly on an allowance from the Elector"?[18] But that was not her style. She was a driven woman, a type A personality, and she simply could not be held back. Imagine her sitting in a rocker, knitting potholders for the rest of her life. Other women, perhaps. Not Katie. She was bound and determined to make her own way and to retain at least de facto guardianship of her four children. She was tenacious, and in the end, she prevailed. But her life was more harried than it had been when her husband was alive. In fact, during the years after Martin's death, she was in court on three different occasions to demand her legal rights.

Only months after Luther had died, Catholic forces faced off against Protestants in what became known as the Schmalkaldic War. "The forces of John Frederick of Saxony and Philip of Hesse," writes Scott Hendrix, "were no match for the troops assembled by Charles and his brother Ferdinand, and in April of 1547 the Lutherans surrendered at Mühlberg,"[19] a town about a day's journey from Wittenberg. Soon thereafter Wittenberg itself became a battleground, Electors Philip and John Frederick having been taken prisoner.

In the midst of this chaos in 1546, with hand-to-hand combat now coming to the streets of Wittenberg, Katie and her three youngest children fled to the fortified town of Magdeburg, soon to be joined by the Melanchthons. That town, however, was swarming with other refugees and was itself not considered safe. So as soon as she learned that the troops had moved on, she returned to Wittenberg, no doubt fearing that her claim on the Black Cloister might be weakened if she were not living in it. During her short absence, however, her fields had been blackened, cattle killed and consumed, gardens in ruins, buildings except for the Black Cloister burned to the ground.[20]

Again in 1547, she and the children were on the road, this time escorted by Philip Melanchthon and heading for Copenhagen, hoping that the king of Denmark would provide support and a safe haven. But the nearly four hundred miles of travel were dangerous and expensive. Long before they reached their destination, they encountered enemy troops, forcing them to turn back. She and the children found safety in a small German town, where they remained for two months before returning to Wittenberg, finding it still in turmoil. In fact, there was no place to hide. Others had panicked and were on the run as well. But one wonders if Katie, amid her fears and deep grief, was simply not making wise choices.

Today we would counsel a widow against making life-altering decisions too soon after the death of a spouse. But even if Katie had been offered such counsel, crop destruction caused by war and bad weather only added to her indecisiveness. We now know that confusion and exhaustion are common symptoms of grief. Indeed, in the year following her husband's death, she was burdened with cares almost beyond her ability to cope.

Before the winter of 1547 set in, the little family had returned to Wittenberg. "It is certain that the double flight exhausted the cash reserves," writes Martin Treu, so much so that she "stood temporarily at the edge of bankruptcy."[21] In these months of uncertainty, Philip Melanchthon, as guardian, stepped in to help out, but his friendship with Katie had never been close. Indeed, Melanchthon, who had revered her husband, was now frustrated by her independence and indecisiveness. And she no doubt felt equally frustrated that she was obliged to depend on him. But after a time, when she was able to gain legal control of her Zülsdorf property (with Melanchthon's help), she had apparently regained some financial stability.

It is interesting that, amid her deep grief, Katie had assumed that her only real financial security depended on accumulating more land, as the purchase of a farm at Wachsdorf demonstrated. But hard times were only a harvest away, and in order to make ends meet, she would later have to mortgage her beloved Zülsdorf. Yet she persevered, and through her persistence and chutzpah, her sons were granted scholarships, the money provided by court officials whose loyalty to Luther was only grudgingly extended to her.

But for every step forward, it seemed as though she were taking two steps back. Indeed, it appeared as though everything were falling to pieces—her husband dead, his Reformation reduced to torn-up tracts, and now to see all of her own hard work demolished. On top of this was the fact that she had lost her status. While her husband was alive, she was recognized (though often resented) as the wife of the great Reformer. Now she was almost forgotten.

If widowhood, property destruction, and financial troubles had been all Katie had to contend with, her life might have stretched on for decades. Unlike her husband, she was strong, healthy, and mentally stable. We imagine her visiting her children and helping with grand-children. How could anything else go wrong? Yes, of course, a plague was ravaging the land. We plead for her. Hadn't she suffered enough already? Indeed, if she had not yet become a confirmed pessimist by this time, her final months would plunge her into that cold grip of despair.

In addition to owning properties, she had been modestly supported by her late husband's benefactors, including Philip Melanchthon and the king of Denmark, as well as the Duke of Prussia. But the one-time nest egg was gone. When her husband died, they were relatively affluent, thanks to her hard work and her frugality. On that score, her husband died in peace, never imagining that in such a short time, his wife would become a beggar with a *bitter living*. For the last five years of her life, she would plead for money from benefactors, though often without success. Yet she soldiered on, keeping her Black Cloister boardinghouse open, though barely making a profit. Early in 1552, she finally did receive help from the king of Denmark, money she sorely needed to plant her crops—farmer that she was to the end.

But the harvest of 1552 ended badly. Imperial troops were not only ravaging the land, but, as rumor had it, were also spreading disease. When the fury of the plague came to Wittenberg in 1552, conditions were so threatening that by August, the university actually picked up and moved south to Torgau. Katie stayed on to protect her property and bring in the harvest. Soon thereafter, however, fearing that the plague had infected the Black Cloister, she too fled to Torgau.

The final horrific ordeal she faced was her last. With her younger children Paul and Margareta (the older boys away at school), she set out for Torgau. Exactly what happened is uncertain, but the horses bolted. She apparently was either thrown off or jumped from the wagon in an effort to control the horses, and in the process she took a serious fall, landing in a ditch and injuring her back.[22] Imagine her body wracked with serious cuts and bruises and perhaps broken bones and internal injuries. The final painful months were truly sad. Martin had colleagues and friends in the town of Torgau, but they did not step forward to help Katie in her time of need.[23] Daughter Margareta, now eighteen, tried to relieve her mother's severe pain and nurse her back to health, but to no avail. Katharina died some three months later, on December 20, 1552. She was only fifty-three years old.

Her funeral, conducted by Philip Melanchthon and the local rector, was in Torgau. The death notice recognized her as the "wife of the venerable Doctor Martin Luther," but also referred to her own lack of veneration: "Besides the trials of widowhood, she also experienced much ingratitude by many people of whom she should expect help and support for the sake of her husband's public merits in the service of the church, but was often disgracefully disappointed."[24]

What a sorry obituary it was. After all she had accomplished on her own merits apart from being married to the "venerable" doctor, her children must have been "disgracefully disappointed" in the way the notice was worded. But maybe it would have been inappropriate to say that on her own she accomplished more than did the vast majority of men in the sixteenth century, despite their privilege of gender.

The years of Katie's widowhood are difficult to unravel. During her twenty years of marriage to Martin Luther, she was the recipient of letters, and her life parallels his. But after his death, she appears to go missing for months, almost years, at a time. Some aspects of her life and responses to her husband's death remain in the realm of mystery. In fact, one such mystery relates to a 1546 woodcut depicting her in mourning. Her mouth is covered by a piece of cloth. Some have speculated that the bandaged mouth was to represent the silence a widow should maintain in the absence of a husband who was to rule over her. Susan Karant-Nunn has pointed out that as late as the sixteenth century, widows were portrayed with clothing covering their mouths—"a symbolic representation of *mundtod* ("deadmouth"), the legal principle by which medieval German widows were denied a legal voice or identity." They were to be represented by a male relative.[25]

Katie would have scorned the idea of a mouth covering. The only one she would have ever worn would have been found in a woodcut, surely not on her person. But pictures tell us a lot about the times. Another interesting piece of art that also appeared in 1546, the year of Luther's death, is titled *The Fountain of Youth.* Painted by Lucas Cranach the Elder, it speaks volumes about the tenor of the times. While I will always be grateful for his painting of Katie (though the facial features of his women often have a similar flat and expressionless look), this piece is much more interesting and is entertaining as well.

The fountain of youth is a swimming pool of sorts in the center of the painting. Old women (most likely widows with no hope of a second marriage) are being carted and carried to the edge of the pool in various stages of undress. Indeed, naked, with breasts hanging low, they cautiously step down into the water. The ones already in the pool, who are standing and swimming, have a distinct appearance of youth. And by the time they are stepping out on the other side, they are nubile, naked maidens. From there, they enter a dressing room and emerge in beautiful ball gowns, one of the women partially hidden in the bushes—doing who knows what—with a handsome gentleman.[26]

Here Cranach is having a good time with his paintbrushes, and the piece of art just happens to appear the same year that Katie, who twenty years earlier had lived in his home, became a widow. It is doubtful she ever saw the painting, and if she had, she would have found it scandalous. The thought of being a youthful forty-seven (as she was when she was widowed) was ludicrous. Life and death were real, with no time for fanciful fountains of youth.

What a terrible tragedy it was that her life ended so soon! She would never cuddle with grandchildren or live to see that her husband's legacy was as secure as were his books and tracts. The more they were burned, the faster they appeared in new printings and translations. Luther's reform was part of a larger movement spreading far beyond the borders of Germany that simply could not be stopped. Indeed, there were glimmers of hope that diplomacy might prevail and war averted. In fact, in 1555, three years after Katie died, tentative steps toward religious toleration were set in place with the Peace of Augsburg. With that agreement, each of the German rulers could choose whether his territory would be Catholic or Lutheran. Though religious conflict would surely continue, it was a stunning accord that seemed almost unthinkable during Martin Luther's lifetime.

As it was, Katie's last seven years were fraught with disaster and discrimination. She was stuck in the 1540s. There was no five-hundredth anniversary to look back on. She could not have comprehended that one day, far in the future, there might be a grand, yearlong commemoration. And Katie? Her life would be wrung dry by writers in search of sufficient words for a biography. She did not have the peaceful death that the record shows for her husband. Did she rage, rage against the final dying, dimming light, as Dylan Thomas profoundly expressed in his familiar poem?[27]

Was she raging in her sick bed and, in those last days and hours, knowing there were too many tasks left undone—and children left unmothered?

Brand Bora

CONCLUDING THOUGHTS
ON KATHARINA

Not knowing Katharina von Bora is a key to knowing her. Understanding is sometimes found in obscurity. What we do know of her comes largely through her husband's writings, thus seeing her in his reflection. Or perhaps knowing her as we know black holes— not by seeing them, but by knowing their effects on nearby matter. So it is with Katie. We see her primarily through her husband's reflections and by her effects on others. And as such we do see her. We see her, albeit "through a glass darkly," to quote the apostle Paul (1 Corinthians 13:12 KJV).

A valid question might be this: Can one write a biography of a black hole? Of a person seen only through a glass darkly? "A real biography of Katharina von Bora could hardly be written even in the future," writes Martin Treu. "The base of sources is too small. Her eight extant letters, none of them in her own hand, are all concerned with economic projects."[1]

Treu's last two words—"economic projects"—are a dead giveaway. What we know about Katie relates largely to her business dealings, primarily gleaned from Luther's letters to her and to others. And this is the key to knowing Katie. As the wife of Martin Luther, she was certainly known by her contemporaries and particularly Luther's colleagues and students. *Why then*, we wonder, *does she not surface significantly in contemporary sources? Why would she be relegated to the black hole of history?*

Was gender the primary factor? Unlikely. In fact, if Katie were just a successful business*man* in Wittenberg, we could easily understand the invisibility. But as Martin Luther's most intimate partner and lover, her gender was a requisite—the very reason for her significance. So we conclude the issue was not wrong gender. Rather, wrong personality and pursuits—and those two combined with her lack of piety.

Imagine a runaway nun, wretched and impoverished, arriving in Wittenberg in 1523, known for good works and devotion, standing strong for the evangelical gospel, leading women's prayer and Bible study groups, gaining a reputation for godliness, bearing babies who grow up to follow in their father's footsteps. Then we would have all the sources needed for a full biography of the wife of the celebrated Martin Luther. But alas, it would not be Katie.

The most recognizable name of the Reformation was Martin Luther. There were other brand names, but his outranked them all. Brand Luther, according to Andrew Pettegree, incorporated many things, not the least of which was an evangelical gospel drawn directly from Paul's epistles. And Brand Luther also stood for "The Nation's Pastor" (a chapter title in Pettegree's book, *Brand Luther*). Luther was known, not only as the courageous Reformer who had stood strong against the powerful Catholic Church, but also as a counselor and friend who refused to become rich peddling the gospel: "he preferred to make no money from his books, written always in God's cause, and to give no further ammunition to his enemies by profiteering from God's work."[2]

This was all Brand Luther, and Brand Luther sold—every spoken and written word—whether or not he profited.

Brand Bora did not. This is a critical factor in understanding Katharina. Pettegree further observes (in relation to Luther's refusal to take profits from his books) that "he could now well afford this high-mindedness, thanks partly to his businesswoman wife, who kept the household well provided for and brought in considerable extra income from her various business ventures."[3]

Brand Bora did not sell. Her brand was resented by many, including Luther's closest colleagues. Brand Bora stood for businesswoman. Indeed, Katie was branded—branded as an independent, driven, and secular woman. If Martin's brand was in part the nation's pastor, hers was *not* the nation's pastor's wife. Then, as now, that role came with unwritten requirements. Had she been deeply devout, known primarily for piety and unswerving support of her husband's evangelical reform, might Brand Bora sources be plentiful? Might the biographer's task be easier?

As it was, her husband's contemporaries and his followers in the next generation essentially branded her into obscurity. Take her out of the equation, however, and we would be looking at a very different Reformation. Take away her profound influence on her husband, and Brand Luther would have been seriously diminished.

Notes

Introduction: Katharina von Bora for All Seasons

1. See Ruth A. Tucker, *Extraordinary Women of Christian History: What We Can Learn from Their Struggles and Triumphs* (Grand Rapids: Baker, 2016), 24.
2. Drafting Committee of the LCWE, "Christian Witness to Nominal Christians among Roman Catholics," Lausanne Occasional Paper 10 (June 1980), www.lausanne.org/content/lop/lop-10 (accessed December 1, 2016).
3. John R. W. Stott, *Basic Christianity* (London: Inter-Varsity, 1958), 108.
4. Drafting Committee of the LCWE, "Christian Witness to Nominal Christians."
5. Jeanette C. Smith, "Katharina von Bora through Five Centuries: A Historiography," *Sixteenth Century Journal* 30.3 (1999): 745.

Chapter 1: "Jesus Cage"

1. Casey N. Cep, "Inside the Cloister," *New Yorker*, March 5, 2014, www.newyorker.com/books/page-turner/inside-the-cloister.
2. Ibid.
3. Laurel Braswell, "Saint Edburga of Winchester: A Study of Her Cult, A.D. 950–1500," *Medieval Studies* 23 (1971): 310.
4. See Eileen Power, *Medieval English Nunneries* (Cambridge: Cambridge University Press, 1922), 25.
5. See Martin Treu, "Katharina von Bora, the Woman at Luther's Side," *Lutheran Quarterly* 13 (summer 1999): 157, www.lutheranquarterly.com/uploads/7/4/0/1/7401289/treu_katharina_von_bora.pdf (accessed December 1, 2016).
6. Cited in Rudolf K. Markwald and Marilynn Morris Markwald, *Katharina von Bora: A Reformation Life* (St. Louis, MO: Concordia, 2002), 24.
7. Martin Brecht, *Martin Luther: Shaping and Defining the Reformation, 1521–1532*, trans. James L. Schaaf (Minneapolis: Fortress, 1990), 101.
8. Heide Wunder, *He Is the Sun, She Is the Moon: Women in Early Modern Germany* (Cambridge, MA: Harvard University Press, 1998), 17.
9. See Anne Winston-Allen, *Convent Chronicles: Women Writing about Women and Reform in the Late Middle Ages* (University Park: Pennsylvania State University Press, 2004), 29, 45, 49.
10. Judith Oliver, "Worship and the Word," in *Women and the Book: Assessing the Visual Evidence*, ed. Jane H. M. Taylor and Lesley Smith (London: University of Toronto Press, 1996), 106.
11. Ibid., 107.
12. See Ernst Kroker, *The Mother of the Reformation: The Amazing Life and Story of Katharine Luther*, trans. Mark E. DeGarmeaux (St. Louis, MO: Concordia, 2013), 19.

13. Hildegard von Bingen, "Her Life: Work as Abbess / Richardis of Stade," http//land derhildegard.de/her-life-work-as-abbess-richardis-of-stade (accessed December 1, 2016).

14. Ulrike Wiethaus, "In Search of Medieval Women's Friendships: Hildegard of Bingen's Letters to Her Female Contemporaries," in Ulrike Wiethaus, ed., *Maps of Flesh and Light: The Religious Experience of Medieval Women Mystics* (Syracuse, NY: Syracuse University Press, 1993), 106.

15. Joseph L. Baird and Radd K. Ehrman, trans., *The Letters of Hildegard of Bingen*, vol. 1 (New York: Oxford University Press, 1994), 51.

16. Quoted in Winston-Allen, *Convent Chronicles*, 129–30.

17. Cited in Markwald and Markwald, *Katherina von Bora*, 40.

18. Cited in Lina Eckenstein, *Woman under Monasticism* (London: Clay, 1896), 67–68.

19. Ibid.

20. Cited in Christian D. Knudsen, *Naughty Nuns and Promiscuous Monks: Monastic Sexual Misconduct in Late Medieval England* (University of Toronto, PhD dissertation, 2012), 97–99, https://tspace.library.utoronto.ca/bitstream/1807/67281/6/Knudsen_Christian_D_201211_PhD_thesis.pdf (accessed December 1, 2016).

21. Martin Luther King Jr., "I Have a Dream," speech at the "March on Washington" (August 28, 1963), https://kinginstitute.stanford.edu/king-papers/documents/i-have-dream-address-delivered-march-washington-jobs-and-freedom (accessed December 1, 2016).

22. Quoted in Winston-Allen, *Convent Chronicles*, 233.

23. Quoted in Thomas A. Brady, *German Histories in the Age of the Reformations, 1400–1650* (New York: Cambridge University Press, 2009), 174.

24. Ibid.

25. "The Plays of Roswitha: Dulcitius," Fordham University, http://sourcebooks.fordham.edu/basis/roswitha-dulcitius.asp (accessed December 1, 2016).

26. Winston-Allen, *Convent Chronicles*, 22.

27. Cited in ibid., 24.

28. Ibid., 25.

29. Ibid.

30. Treu, "Katharina von Bora," 158.

31. Patricia O'Donnell-Gibson, *The Red Skirt: Memoirs of an Ex Nun* (Watervliet, MI: StuartRose, 2011), 38.

32. Ibid., 85.

33. Cited in Markwald and Markwald, *Katharina von Bora*, 40.

Chapter 2: "Here I Stand"

1. Tom Browning, "A History of the Reformation: "The Door . . . Martin Luther," December 19, 2003, www.monergism.com/thethreshold/articles/onsite/browning/Lesson8.pdf (accessed December 1, 2016).

2. Quoted in Timothy George, *Theology of the Reformers*, rev. ed. (Nashville: Broadman & Holman, 2013), 88.

3. Quoted in Joel F. Harrington, *The Faithful Executioner: Life and Death, Honor and Shame in the Turbulent Sixteenth Century* (New York: Farrar, Straus and Giroux, 2013), 33.

4. Quoted in Lewis Spitz, ed., *Luther's Works*, vol. 34 (Philadelphia: Muhlenberg, 1960), 337.

5. Quoted in Martin Marty, *Martin Luther* (New York: Viking, 2004), 6.

6. Quoted in George, *Theology of the Reformers*, 53.

7. John Wesley, *Journal of John Wesley*, Christian Classics Ethereal Library, www.ccel.org/ccel/wesley/journal.vi.ii.xvi.html (accessed December 1, 2016).

8. Quoted in George, *Theology of the Reformers*, 65.

9. Ibid., 63.
10. Quoted in Thomas M. Lindsay, *Luther and the German Reformation* (Edinburgh: T&T Clark, 1900), 50, https://archive.org/stream/luthergermanrefo00lind/luthergerman refo00lind_djvu.txt (accessed December 1, 2016).
11. Karl Barth, *Die christliche Dogmatik im Entwurf: Die Lehre vom Worte Gottes* (Munich: Chr. Kaiser Verlag, 1927), ix.
12. Roland Bainton, *Here I Stand: A Life of Martin Luther* (Nashville: Abingdon, 1950), 60.
13. Quoted in ibid., 147.
14. Quoted in ibid., 185; Bainton writes, "The earliest printed version added the words: 'Here I stand, I cannot do otherwise.' The words, though not recorded on the spot, may nevertheless be genuine, because the listeners at the moment may have been too moved to write."
15. Quoted in Roland H. Bainton, *Women of the Reformation in Germany and Italy* (Minneapolis: Augsburg, 1971), 65.
16. Ibid., 106.
17. Cited in Rudolf K. Markwald and Marilynn Morris Markwald, *Katharina von Bora: A Reformation Life* (St. Louis, MO: Concordia, 2002), 40.
18. Quoted in Jean Rilliet, *Zwingli: Third Man of the Reformation*, trans. Harold Knight (Philadelphia: Westminster, 1964), 33.
19. Kimberly C. Kennedy, "'God's Recurring Dream': Assessing the New Monastic Movement through Historical Comparison" (master's thesis, Olivet Nazarene University, 2012), 14, http://digitalcommons.olivet.edu/cgi/viewcontent.cgi?article =1002&context=hist_maph (accessed December 1, 2016).

Chapter 3: "A Wagon Load of Vestal Virgins"

1. Patricia O'Donnell-Gibson, *The Red Skirt: Memoirs of an Ex Nun* (Watervliet, MI: StuartRose, 2011), 38.
2. Quoted in Roland Bainton, *Here I Stand: A Life of Martin Luther* (Nashville: Abingdon, 1950), 45.
3. J. H. Alexander, "Katherine von Bora, Wife of Luther," www.the-highway.com/article Nov01.html (accessed December 1, 2016).
4. Boise State University, *Martin Luther*, "Luther Marries," 17, https://europeanhistory .boisestate.edu/reformation/luther/17.shtml (accessed December 1, 2016).
5. Armin Stein, *Katharine von Bora, Dr. Martin Luther's Wife: A Picture from Life*, trans. A. Endlich (Philadelphia: General Council Publication Board, 1915), 21.
6. Ibid., 35–37, 40–41.
7. See Scott Hendrix, *Martin Luther: Visionary Reformer* (New Haven, CT: Yale University Press, 2015), 143.
8. Quoted in Bainton, *Here I Stand*, 286–87.
9. Michael Baker, "Was Luther Really Like, After All?" www.catholicapologetics.info/ apologetics/protestantism/character.htm (accessed December 1, 2016).
10. Theodore Gerhardt Tappert, ed., *Luther: Letters of Spiritual Counsel* (Philadelphia: Westminster, 1955), 172.
11. Ernst Kroker, *The Mother of the Reformation: The Amazing Life and Story of Katharine Luther*, trans. Mark E. DeGarmeaux (St. Louis, MO: Concordia, 2013), 40.
12. Ibid.
13. Eileen Power, *Medieval English Nunneries: c. 1275–1535* (Cambridge: Cambridge University Press, 1922), 36.
14. Preserved Smith and Charles M. Jacobs, eds., *Luther's Correspondence and Other Contemporary Letters*, vol. 2 (Philadelphia: Lutheran Publication Society, 1918), 258.

15. Steven Ozment, *The Serpent and the Lamb: Cranach, Luther, and the Making of the Reformation* (New Haven, CT: Yale University Press, 2011), 271.

16. James Anderson, *Ladies of the Reformation* (New York: Blackie, 1858), 55.

17. Quoted in Martin Treu, "Katharina von Bora, the Woman at Luther's Side," *Lutheran Quarterly* 13 (summer 1999): 176, note 3, www.lutheranquarterly.com/uploads/7/4/0/1/7401289/treu_katharina_von_bora.pdf (accessed December 1, 2016).

18. Quoted in Hendrix, *Martin Luther*, 142.

19. Smith and Jacobs, eds., *Luther's Correspondence*, 2:181.

20. Ibid.

21. See Susan C. Karant-Nunn and Merry E. Wiesner-Hanks, eds., *Luther on Women* (New York: Cambridge University Press, 2003), 132.

22. Quoted in Roland Bainton, "Psychiatry and History," in *Psychohistory and Religion: The Case of Young Man Luther*, ed. Roger A. Johnson (Philadelphia: Fortress, 1977), 44.

23. Arthur Cushman McGiffert, *Martin Luther: The Man and His Work* (New York: Century, 1911), 277–78.

24. Glenn Sunshine, "Katharine von Bora," *Christian Worldview Journal*, October 26, 2015, www.colsoncenter.org/the-center/columns/changed/23137-katharina-von-bora (accessed December 1, 2016).

25. Preserved Smith, *The Life and Letters of Martin Luther* (Boston: Houghton Mifflin, 1911), 176.

26. Ibid.

27. Ibid.

28. Quoted in Clyde L. Manschreck, *Melanchthon: The Quiet Reformer* (Eugene, OR: Wipf & Stock, 2009), 129–30.

29. Quoted in Marjorie Elizabeth Plummer, *From Priest's Whore to Pastor's Wife: Clerical Marriage and the Progress of Reform in the Early German Reformation* (Burlington, VT: Ashgate, 2012), 51–52.

30. Cited in Justin Taylor, "Martin Luther's Reform of Marriage," in *Sex and the Supremacy of Christ*, eds. John Piper and Justin Taylor (Wheaton, IL: Crossway, 2005), 223.

31. Cited in Roland H. Bainton, *Women of the Reformation in Germany and Italy* (Minneapolis: Augsburg, 1971), 24.

Chapter 4: "A Bitter Living"

1. Sheilagh C. Ogilvie, *A Bitter Living: Women, Markets, and Social Capital in Early Modern Germany* (New York: Oxford University Press, 2003), 1.

2. Tim Lambert, "A Brief History of Toilets," *Washingtonian Magazine* (last revised, 2016), www.localhistories.org/toilets.html (accessed December 1, 2016).

3. Ibid.

4. Ibid.

5. Ibid.

6. See Gottfried Krüger, "How Did the Town of Wittenberg Look at the Time of Luther," trans. Holger Sonntag, http://thewittenbergproject.org/about/how-did-the-town-of-wittenberg-look-at-the-time-of-luther (accessed December 1, 2016).

7. Quoted in ibid.

8. Roland Bainton, *Here I Stand: A Life of Martin Luther* (Nashville: Abingdon, 1950), 298.

9. Krüger, "How Did the Town of Wittenberg Look?"

10. See ibid.

11. Quoted in Olli-Pekka Vainio, ed., *Engaging Luther: A (New) Theological Assessment* (Eugene, OR: Wipf & Stock, 2010), 187.

12. See Krüger, "How Did the Town of Wittenberg Look?"
13. Desiderius Erasmus, "On the Education of Children," in *The Erasmus Reader*, ed. Erika Rummel (Toronto: University of Toronto Press, 2003), 73.
14. See Krüger, "How Did the Town of Wittenberg Look?"
15. Wolfgang Capito, "The Frankfurt Book Fair: Part I" (1501), https://wolfgangcapito.wordpress.com/2011/07/07/the-frankfurt-book-fair-part-1 (accessed December 1, 2016).
16. Ibid.
17. Preserved Smith, *The Life and Letters of Martin Luther* (Boston: Houghton Mifflin, 1911), 363.
18. Ogilvie, *A Bitter Living*, 1.
19. Ibid., 10.
20. Ibid.
21. Joel F. Harrington, *The Faithful Executioner: Life and Death, Honor and Shame in the Turbulent Sixteenth Century* (New York: Farrar, Straus and Giroux, 2013), 5.
22. Quoted in Euan Cameron, *Enchanted Europe: Superstition, Reason, and Religion, 1250–1750* (Oxford: Oxford University Press, 2011), 2.
23. Ibid, 3–4.
24. C. Scott Dixon, *The Reformation and Rural Society: The Parishes of Brandenburg-Ansbach-Kulmbach, 1528–1603* (Cambridge: Cambridge University Press, 1996), 102.
25. Harrington, *Faithful Executioner*, 33.
26. Ibid., 6.
27. Ibid., 5.
28. Quoted in ibid., 8.
29. Cited in Smith, *Life and Letters of Martin Luther*, 361.
30. Cited in ibid., 362.
31. Cited in ibid.
32. Saint Teresa, *The Life of Teresa of Jesus* (1888; repr., New York: Garden City, NY, 1960), lxvii.
33. Quoted in Susan Broomhall, *Women and the Book Trade in Sixteenth-Century France* (Hampshire, UK: Ashgate, 2002), 2.
34. Ann Marie Rasmussen, *Mothers and Daughters in Medieval German Literature* (Syracuse, NY: Syracuse University Press, 1997), 204.

Chapter 5: "Pigtails on the Pillow"

1. Quoted in Marjorie Elizabeth Plummer, *From Priest's Whore to Pastor's Wife* (Burlington, VT: Ashgate, 2012), 126.
2. Quoted in Philip Schaff, *History of the Christian Church*, vol. 7 (Grand Rapids: Eerdmans, 1979), 455.
3. Quoted in William Herman Theodore, ed., *Four Hundred Years: Commemorative Essays on the Reformation of Dr. Martin Luther and Its Blessed Results* (St. Louis, MO: Concordia, 1916), 143.
4. Quoted in Richard Friedenthal, *Luther: His Life and Times*, trans. John Nowell (New York: Harcourt Brace Jovanovich, 1970), 438.
5. Patrick F. O'Hare, *The Facts about Luther* (Cincinnati, OH: Pustet, 1916), 353.
6. Quoted in Preserved Smith, *The Life and Letters of Martin Luther* (Boston: Houghton Mifflin, 1911), 130.
7. Cited in Carter Lindberg, "Martin Luther on Marriage and the Family," 30, www.emanuel.ro/wp-content/uploads/2014/06/P-2.1-2004-Carter-Lindberg-Martin-Luther-on-Marriage-and-the-Family.pdf (accessed December 1, 2016).

8. See Helen L. Parish, *Clerical Celibacy in the West, c. 1100–1700* (Burlington, VT: Ashgate, 2010), 146.

9. Ibid., 147.

10. See William Lazareth, *Luther on the Christian Home: An Application of the Social Ethics of the Reformation* (Philadelphia: Muhlenberg, 1960), 23.

11. Quoted in ibid.

12. Ibid.

13. Ibid., 22.

14. Ibid.

15. Quoted in Robert Dean Linder, *The Reformation Era* (Westport, CT: Greenwood, 2008), 26.

16. See Lazareth, *Luther on the Christian Home,* 21.

17. Gregory of Tours, *The History of the Franks,* trans. Lewis Thorpe (London: Penguin, 1974), 74–75.

18. Preserved Smith and Charles M. Jacobs, eds., *Luther's Correspondence and Other Contemporary Letters* (Philadelphia: Lutheran Publication Society, 1918), 2:326.

19. Cited in Rudolf K. Markwald and Marilynn Morris Markwald, *Katharina von Bora: A Reformation Life* (St. Louis, MO: Concordia, 2002), 78.

20. Quoted in Heiko Oberman, *Luther, Man Between God and the Devil* (New York: Doubleday, 1982), 282.

21. Quoted in Moritz Meurer, *The Life of Martin Luther: Related from Original Authorities* (New York: Ludwig, 1848), 320-21.

22. Ernst Kroker, *The Mother of the Reformation: The Amazing Life and Story of Katharine Luther,* trans. Mark E. DeGarmeaux (St. Louis, MO: Concordia, 2013), 73.

23. Quoted in Roland H. Bainton, *Women of the Reformation in Germany and Italy* (Minneapolis: Augsburg, 1971), 27.

24. See Anne Winston-Allen, *Convent Chronicles: Women Writing about Women and Reform in the Late Middle Ages* (University Park: Pennsylvania State University Press, 2004), 233.

25. Quoted in Sabina Flanagan, *Hildegard of Bingen, 1098–1179: A Visionary Life,* 2nd ed. (New York: Routledge, 1998), 70.

26. See Martin Treu, "Katharina von Bora, the Woman at Luther's Side," *Lutheran Quarterly* 13 (summer 1999): 159, www.lutheranquarterly.com/uploads/7/4/0/1/7401289/treu_katharina_von_bora.pdf (accessed December 1, 2016).

27. See ibid.

28. Martin Brecht, *Martin Luther: Shaping and Defining the Reformation,* 1521–1532, trans. James L. Schaaf (Minneapolis: Fortress, 1990), 202–3.

29. Ibid., 203.

30. Ibid.

31. Ibid., 202.

32. Ibid.

33. Andrew Pettegree, *Brand Luther: 1517, Printing, and the Making of the Reformation* (New York: Penguin, 2015), 253.

34. Heinrich Denifle, *Luther and Lutherdom,* trans. Raymund Volz (Somerset, UK: Torch, 1917), 312.

35. Ibid., 313.

36. Quoted in Bainton, *Women of the Reformation,* 23.

37. See Roland Bainton, *Here I Stand: A Life of Martin Luther* (Nashville: Abingdon, 1950), 308.

38. Marjorie Elizabeth Plummer, *From Priest's Whore to Pastor's Wife: Clerical Marriage and the Progress of Reform in the Early German Reformation* (Burlington, VT: Ashgate, 2012), 247.

39. Laurel Thatcher Ulrich, *Well-Behaved Women Seldom Make History* (New York: Knopf, 2007), xiii.

Chapter 6: "Neither Wood nor Stone"

1. Quoted in Michael Parsons, *Reformation Marriage: The Husband and Wife Relationship in the Theology of Luther and Calvin* (Eugene, OR: Wipf & Stock, 2011), 1.

2. Quoted in Roland H. Bainton, *Women of the Reformation in Germany and Italy* (Minneapolis: Augsburg, 1971), 29.

3. Quoted in Ernst Kroker, *The Mother of the Reformation: The Amazing Life and Story of Katharine Luther*, trans. Mark E. DeGarmeaux (St. Louis, MO: Concordia, 2013), 264.

4. See Barbara Hudson Powers, *The Henrietta Mears Story* (Grand Rapids: Revell, 1957), 191.

5. Quoted in Martin Marty, *Martin Luther* (New York: Penguin, 2004), vii.

6. James Reston Jr., *Luther's Fortress: Martin Luther and His Reformation Under Siege* (New York: Basic Books, 2015), 85.

7. Roland Bainton, *Here I Stand: A Life of Martin Luther* (Nashville: Abingdon, 1950), 293.

8. Susan Squire, *I Don't: A Contrarian History of Marriage* (New York: Bloomsbury, 2008), 210.

9. Quoted in Reston, *Luther's Fortress*, 88.

10. Ibid.

11. Quoted in Susan C. Karant-Nunn and Merry E. Wiesner-Hanks, eds., *Luther on Women* (New York: Cambridge University Press, 2003), 120.

12. Cited in Leland Ryken, *Worldly Saints: The Puritans as They Really Were* (Grand Rapids: Zondervan, 1986), 73.

13. See William Lazareth, *Luther on the Christian Home: An Application of the Social Ethics of the Reformation* (Philadelphia: Muhlenberg, 1960), 145.

14. Ibid.

15. Cited in Timothy J. Wengert, ed., *Harvesting Martin Luther's Reflections on Theology, Ethics, and the Church* (Grand Rapids: Eerdmans, 2004), 13–14.

16. Ibid., 13.

17. Quoted in Margaret A. Currie, ed., *The Letters of Martin Luther* (New York: Macmillan, 1908), xii.

18. Quoted in Carter Lindberg, "Martin Luther on Marriage and the Family," 32, www .emanuel.ro/wp-content/uploads/2014/06/P-2.1-2004-Carter-Lindberg-Martin-Luther -on-Marriage-and-the-Family.pdf (accessed December 1, 2016).

19. Ibid., 33.

20. Quoted in Preserved Smith, *The Life and Letters of Martin Luther* (Boston: Houghton Mifflin, 1911), 251.

21. Quoted in Andrew Pettegree, *Brand Luther: 1517, Printing, and the Making of the Reformation* (New York: Penguin, 2015), 261.

22. See Currie, ed., *Letters of Martin Luther*, 361.

23. Quoted in H. C. Erik Midelfort, *A History of Madness in Sixteenth-Century Germany* (Stanford, CA: Stanford University Press, 1999), 106.

24. Ibid., 104.

25. See Martin Brecht, *Martin Luther: Shaping and Defining the Reformation*, 1521–1532, trans. James L. Schaaf (Minneapolis: Fortress, 1990), 210.

26. Quoted in Philip Schaff, *History of the Christian Church* (Grand Rapids: Eerdmans, 1979), 7:337–38.

27. See Smith, *Life and Letters of Martin Luther*, 341.
28. See Karant-Nunn and Wiesner-Hanks, *Luther on Women*, 178–79.
29. Quoted in Smith, *Life and Letters of Martin Luther*, 324.
30. Ibid.
31. See ibid., 341.
32. Ibid.
33. William Keddie, ed., *The Sabbath School Magazine*, vol. 36 (Glasgow: Glasgow Sabbath School Union, 1884), 240.
34. Quoted in *Punch, or the London Charivari*, vol. 30 (London: Bradbury and Agnew, 1856), 99.
35. Quoted in Julius Köstlin, *The Life of Martin Luther* (Philadelphia: Lutheran Publication Society, 1883), 355.
36. Karant-Nunn and Wiesner-Hanks, *Luther on Women*, 9.
37. Ibid., 11–12.
38. Richard Marius, *Martin Luther: The Christian between God and Death* (Cambridge, MA: Harvard University Press, 1999), 439.
39. See Karant-Nunn and Wiesner-Hanks, *Luther on Women*, 12.
40. Bainton, *Here I Stand*, 298.
41. Cited in ibid., 296.
42. Quoted in Clayborne Carson and Kris Shepard, eds., *A Call to Conscience: The Landmark Speeches of Dr. Martin Luther King, Jr.* (New York: Warner, 2002), 66–67.

Chapter 7: "From Katie, a Little Heathen"

1. Sue Hubbell, *A Country Year: Living the Questions* (New York: Houghton Mifflin, 1999), 90.
2. Katy Schumpert, "Why I Am Not a Pastor," March 11, 2015, http://katieluthersisters.org/2015/03/why-i-am-not-a-pastor (viewed March 30, 2016).
3. See Carter Lindberg, "Martin Luther on Marriage and the Family," 29, www.emanuel.ro/wp-content/uploads/2014/06/P-2.1-2004-Carter-Lindberg-Martin-Luther-on-Marriage-and-the-Family.pdf (accessed December 1, 2016).
4. J. A. P. Jones, *Europe, 1500–1600* (Nashville: Nelson, 1997), 75.
5. Ibid.
6. See Martin Treu, "Katharina von Bora, the Woman at Luther's Side," *Lutheran Quarterly* 13 (summer 1999): 163, www.lutheranquarterly.com/uploads/7/4/0/1/7401289/treu_katharina_von_bora.pdf (accessed December 1, 2016).
7. See Henry Barnard, ed., "Early Training: Home Education," *The American Journal of Education*, vol. 8, no. 20, March, 1860 (Hartford, CT: Brownell, 1860), 78.
8. See Roland Bainton, *Here I Stand: A Life of Martin Luther* (Nashville: Abingdon, 1950), 293.
9. Quoted in Roland H. Bainton, *Women of the Reformation in Germany and Italy* (Minneapolis: Augsburg, 1971), 38.
10. See Martin Brecht, *Martin Luther: Shaping and Defining the Reformation*, 1521–1532, trans. James L. Schaaf (Minneapolis: Fortress, 1990), 204.
11. Cited in Bainton, *Here I Stand*, 293.
12. Quoted in Brecht, *Martin Luther*, 204.
13. Ibid.
14. Cited in ibid.
15. See Rudolf K. Markwald and Marilynn Morris Markwald, *Katharina von Bora: A Reformation Life* (St. Louis, MO: Concordia, 2002), 102; see also Peter Matheson, *Argula von Grumbach: A Woman's Voice in the Reformation* (Edinburgh: T&T Clark, 1995), 121–22.
16. Richard Marius, *Martin Luther: The Christian Between God and Death* (Cambridge, MA: Harvard University Press, 1999), 439.

17. See William Lazareth, *Luther on the Christian Home: An Application of the Social Ethics of the Reformation* (Philadelphia: Muhlenberg, 1960), 144.

18. Cited in Philip Schaff and Arthur Gilman, eds., *A Library of Religious Poetry* (New York: Dodd, Mead, 1881), 716.

19. See Lindberg, "Martin Luther on Marriage," 35.

20. See Martin Luther, "A Sermon on the Estate of Marriage," in *Luther's Works*, ed. J. Pelikan and H. T. Lehmann (Saint Louis, MO: Concordia, 1966), 44:8.

21. Quoted in Lazareth, *Luther on the Christian Home*, 144–45.

22. Quoted in Scott H. Hendrix, *Martin Luther: A Very Short Introduction* (New York: Oxford University Press, 2010), 76.

23. Quoted in William Dallmann, ed., *The Lutheran Witness*, vol. 11 (Baltimore, MD: Lang, 1892–1893), 78.

24. Quoted in Ferdinand Piper and H. M. McCracken, eds., *Lives of the Leaders of Our Church Universal* (Chicago: Andrews, 1879), 278.

25. Hendrix, *Martin Luther: A Very Short Introduction*, 77.

26. Ibid.

27. See Treu, "Katharina von Bora," 164.

28. Ibid., 165.

29. Ibid.

30. Ibid.

31. Cited in Susan C. Karant-Nunn and Merry E. Wiesner-Hanks, eds., *Luther on Women* (New York: Cambridge University Press, 2003), 171–72.

32. Susan C. Karant-Nunn, "The Masculinity of Martin Luther: Theory, Practicality, and Humor," in *Masculinity in the Reformation Era*, ed. Scott H. Hendrix and Susan C. Karant-Nunn (Kirksville, MO: Truman State University Press, 2008), 170.

33. Mickey L. Mattox, "Luther on Eve, Women and the Church," in *The Pastoral Luther: Essays on Martin Luther's Practical Theology*, ed. Timothy J. Wengert (Grand Rapids: Eerdmans, 2009), 257.

34. Ibid., 259.

35. Martin Luther, *The Life of Luther, Written by Himself*, ed. M. Michelet (New York: Macmillan, 1904), 262.

Chapter 8: "Morning Star of Wittenberg"

1. Margaret Thatcher, "Speech at Women's International Zionist Organisation Centenary Lunch," May 2, 1990, www.margaretthatcher.org/document/108078 (accessed December 1, 2016).

2. Proverbs 31:10, my paraphrase.

3. Rudolph W. Heinze, *Reform and Conflict: From the Medieval World to the Wars of Religion, A.D. 1350–1648* (Oxford: Monarch, 2006), 111.

4. Sharon Hunt, "In the boarding house," *Culinate*, April 9, 2013.

5. See Preserved Smith, *The Life and Letters of Martin Luther* (Boston: Houghton Mifflin, 1911), 179.

6. Martin Treu, "Katharina von Bora, the Woman at Luther's Side," *Lutheran Quarterly* 13 (summer 1999): 165, www.lutheranquarterly.com/uploads/7/4/0/1/7401289/treu_katharina_von_bora.pdf (accessed December 1, 2016).

7. Quoted in Margaret A. Currie, ed., *The Letters of Martin Luther* (New York: Macmillan, 1908), 299.

8. Cited in Roland Bainton, *Here I Stand: A Life of Martin Luther* (Nashville: Abingdon, 1950), 292.

9. Ibid., 296.

10. Cited in Roland H. Bainton, *Women of the Reformation in Germany and Italy* (Minneapolis: Augsburg, 1971), 32–33.

11. Cited in Treu, "Katharina von Bora," 167–68.

12. Sara Hall, "Katherine von Bora Luther: Herbalist, Gardener, Farmer, and Patron Saint of the Reformation," April 4, 2012, *The Daily Herb*, www.thedailyherb.com/katherine -von-bora-luther-herbalist-gardener-farmer-and-patron-saint-of-the-reformation (accessed December 1, 2016).

13. Bainton, *Here I Stand*, 292.

14. Ibid., 292–93.

15. Steven Ozment, *Ancestors: The Loving Family in Old Europe* (Cambridge, MA: Harvard University Press, 2001), 32.

16. Hall, "Katherine von Bora Luther."

17. Ibid.

18. See ibid.

19. See Ernst Kroker, *The Mother of the Reformation: The Amazing Life and Story of Katharine Luther*, trans. Mark E. DeGarmeaux (St. Louis, MO: Concordia, 2013), 109.

20. See Treu, "Katharina von Bora," 166.

21. Ibid.

22. Quoted in ibid., 168.

23. Ibid., 169.

24. Quoted in Andrew Pettegree, *Brand Luther: 1517, Printing, and the Making of the Reformation* (New York: Penguin, 2015), 272.

25. Richard Marius, *Martin Luther: The Christian Between God and Death* (Cambridge, MA: Harvard University Press, 1999), 439.

26. Quoted in Currie, ed., *Letters of Martin Luther*, 317–18.

27. Ibid., 318.

28. Würzburger Hofbräu Light, *RateBeer*, www.ratebeer.com/beer/wurzburger-hofbrau -light/43802 (accessed December 1, 2016).

29. See Bainton, *Women of the Reformation*, 52.

30. Marius, *Martin Luther*, 440.

Chapter 9: "Hew an Obedient Wife Out of Stone"

1. Mickey L. Mattox, "Luther on Eve, Women and the Church," in *The Pastoral Luther: Essays on Martin Luther's Practical Theology*, ed. Timothy J. Wengert (Grand Rapids: Eerdmans, 2009), 251–52.

2. Quoted in Steven Ozment, *Ancestors: The Loving Family in Old Europe* (Cambridge, MA: Harvard University Press, 2001), 37.

3. Gerhild Scholz Williams, "The Woman/The Witch: Variations on a Sixteenth-Century Theme," in *The Crannied Wall: Women, Religion, and the Arts in Early Modern Europe*, ed. Craig A. Monson (Ann Arbor: University of Michigan Press, 1992), 131.

4. Carolyn Walker Bynum, *Jesus as Mother: Studies in the Spirituality of the High Middle Ages* (Berkeley: University of California Press, 1982), 172–73.

5. Elsie Anne McKee, *Katharina Schütz Zell: The Life and Thought of a Sixteenth-Century Reformer* (Leiden: Brill, 1999), 48.

6. See Susan C. Karant-Nunn and Merry E. Wiesner-Hanks, eds., *Luther on Women* (New York: Cambridge University Press, 2003), 93.

7. Ibid., 94.

8. Quoted in Preserved Smith, *The Life and Letters of Martin Luther* (Boston: Houghton Mifflin, 1911), 180.

9. Ibid.

10. Ibid., 181.

11. Ernst Kroker, *The Mother of the Reformation: The Amazing Life and Story of Katharine Luther,* trans. Mark E. DeGarmeaux (St. Louis, MO: Concordia, 2013), 263.

12. Ibid., 160.

13. Ibid., 161.

14. Ibid., 181.

15. Ibid., 194–95.

16. Quoted in Richard Marius, *Martin Luther: The Christian Between God and Death* (Cambridge, MA: Harvard University Press, 1999), 440.

17. Quoted in Roland H. Bainton, *Women of the Reformation in Germany and Italy* (Minneapolis: Augsburg, 1971), 55.

18. Ibid.

19. Quoted in Smith, *Life and Letters of Martin Luther,* 180.

20. See Bobby Valentine, "Argula von Grumbach: Courageous Debater, Theologian, Female Voice in the Reformation," September 11, 2007, *Wineskins.org,* http://stonedcampbell disciple.com/2007/09/11/argula-von-grumbach-courageous-debater-theologian-female-voice-in-the-reformation-a-woman-on-the-family-tree (accessed December 1, 2016).

21. Marius, *Martin Luther,* 438.

22. Quoted in Smith, *Life and Letters of Martin Luther,* 181.

23. Quoted in Heiko Oberman, *Luther: Man Between God and the Devil,* trans. Eileen Walliser-Schwarzbart (New Haven, CT: Yale University Press, 2006), 276.

24. Quoted in Martin Treu, "Katharina von Bora, the Woman at Luther's Side," *Lutheran Quarterly* 13 (summer 1999): 167, www.lutheranquarterly.com/uploads/7/4/0/1/7401289/treu_katharina_von_bora.pdf (accessed December 1, 2016).

25. Quoted in George H. Tavard, *Women in Christian Tradition* (South Bend, IN: University of Notre Dame Press, 1973), 174.

26. Quoted in Karant-Nunn and Wiesner-Hanks, eds., *Luther on Women,* 190.

27. See ibid., 192–93.

28. Quoted in Rudolf K. Markwald and Marilynn Morris Markwald, *Katharina von Bora: A Reformation Life* (St. Louis, MO: Concordia, 2002), 109.

29. Ibid., 110.

30. See Bainton, *Women of the Reformation,* 29.

31. Quoted in Erin Allen, "Remember the Ladies," *Library of Congress Blog,* March 31, 2016, https://blogs.loc.gov/loc/2016/03/remember-the-ladies (accessed December 1, 2016).

32. Quoted in Woody Holton, *Abigail Adams: A Life* (New York: Simon & Schuster, 2010), 390.

Chapter 10: "Stop Worrying, Let God Worry"

1. Joel F. Harrington, *The Faithful Executioner: Life and Death, Honor and Shame in the Turbulent Sixteenth Century* (New York: Farrar, Straus and Giroux, 2013), 5.

2. Quoted in Preserved Smith, *The Life and Letters of Martin Luther* (Boston: Houghton Mifflin, 1911), 179.

3. Quoted in Dennis Ngien, *Luther as a Spiritual Adviser: The Interface of Theology and Piety in Luther's Devotional Writings* (Eugene, OR: Wipf & Stock, 2007), 78.

4. See Steven Ozment, *When Fathers Ruled: Family Life in Reformation Europe* (Cambridge, MA: Harvard University Press, 1983), 148.

5. Graham C. L. Davey, "What Do We Worry About?" May 21, 2013, *Psychology Today,* www.psychologytoday.com/blog/why-we-worry/201305/what-do-we-worry-about (accessed December 1, 2016).

6. Quoted in Susan C. Karant-Nunn and Merry E. Wiesner-Hanks, eds., *Luther on Women* (New York: Cambridge University Press, 2003), 195.
7. Ibid.
8. Quoted in Martin Luther, *The Life of Luther, Written by Himself,* ed. M. Michelet (New York: Macmillan, 1904), 349.
9. Karant-Nunn and Wiesner-Hanks, *Luther on Women,* 196.
10. Screen observed April 7, 2016.
11. John MacArthur, "A Worried Christian," *Grace to You,* www.gty.org/resources/articles/A112/a-worried-christian (accessed December 1, 2016).
12. Jill Briscoe, "Why Can't I Stop Worrying?" www.womensministrytools.com/womens-bible-studies/304/why-cant-i-stop-worrying (accessed December 1, 2016).
13. Cited in Karant-Nunn and Wiesner-Hanks, eds., *Luther on Women,* 193.
14. Quoted in Margaret A. Currie, ed., *The Letters of Martin Luther* (New York: Macmillan, 1908), 460.
15. See ibid., 461
16. Ibid.
17. Quoted in James A. Nestingen, *Martin Luther: A Life* (Minneapolis: Augsburg, 2003), 66–67.
18. Quoted in Smith, *Life and Letters of Martin Luther,* 371–72.
19. Ibid., 372.
20. Quoted in Roland H. Bainton, *Women of the Reformation in Germany and Italy* (Minneapolis: Augsburg, 1971), 27.
21. Richard Marius, *Martin Luther: The Christian Between God and Death* (Cambridge, MA: Harvard University Press, 1999), 442.
22. Ibid., 443.
23. Ibid., 442.
24. Ibid., 480.
25. Ibid.
26. Quoted in ibid., 481.
27. Martin Brecht, *Martin Luther: Shaping and Defining the Reformation, 1521–1532,* trans. James L. Schaaf (Minneapolis: Fortress, 1990), 210.
28. See ibid., 211.
29. Marius, *Martin Luther,* 480.
30. Ibid., 78.
31. Ibid., 214.
32. Cited in Bainton, *Women of the Reformation,* 30.
33. My paraphrase of Matthew 6:25–34; 11:28.

Chapter 11: "Fifty Gulden" Bible Reading

1. Preserved Smith, *The Life and Letters of Martin Luther* (Boston: Houghton Mifflin, 1911), 179.
2. Rich Deem, "The Proverbs 31 Woman: Why She Is *Not* the Ideal Christian Wife," www.godandscience.org/doctrine/proverbs_31_woman.html (accessed December 1, 2016).
3. Scot McKnight, *The Real Mary: Why Evangelical Christians Can Embrace the Mother of Jesus* (Brewster, MA: Paraclete, 2007), 4.
4. Dorothy Pape, *In Search of God's Ideal Woman* (Downers Grove, IL: InterVarsity, 1976), 53.
5. Smith, *Life and Letters of Martin Luther,* 176.
6. Martin Marty, *Martin Luther* (New York: Viking, 2004), xii.

7. Cited in Roland Bainton, *Here I Stand: A Life of Martin Luther* (Nashville: Abingdon, 1950), 370.

8. Marty, *Martin Luther*, 23–24.

9. Cited in Warren Wiersbe, *50 People Every Christian Should Know: Learning from Spiritual Giants of the Faith* (Grand Rapids: Baker, 2009), 14.

10. Quoted in Vern L. Bullough, Brenda Shelton, and Sarah Slavin, *The Subordinated Sex: A History of Attitudes Toward Women*, rev. ed. (Athens: University of Georgia Press, 1988), 174.

11. Hollie Dermer, "Women of the Reformation: Katharina Von Bora Luther," http:// christinalangella.com/womenofthereformation/women-of-the-reformation-katharina -von-bora-luther-by-hollie-dermer (accessed December 1, 2016).

12. Kirsi Stjerna, *Women and the Reformation* (Malden, MA: Blackwell, 2009), 54.

13. Ibid.

14. See Martin Treu, "Katharina von Bora, the Woman at Luther's Side," *Lutheran Quarterly* 13 (summer 1999): 159, www.lutheranquarterly.com/uploads/7/4/0/1/ 7401289/treu_katharina_von_bora.pdf (accessed December 1, 2016).

15. Rudolf K. Markwald and Marilynn Morris Markwald, *Katharina von Bora: A Reformation Life* (St. Louis, MO: Concordia, 2002), 134.

16. See ibid., 30.

17. Ibid., 33.

18. See Anne Winston-Allen, *Convent Chronicles: Women Writing about Women and Reform in the Late Middle Ages* (University Park: Pennsylvania State University Press, 2004), 133.

19. Ibid.

20. Jo Ann McNamara, *Sisters in Arms: Catholic Nuns through Two Millennia* (Cambridge, MA: Harvard University Press, 1996), 393.

21. Winston-Allen, *Convent Chronicles*, 135.

22. Quoted in Roland H. Bainton, *Women of the Reformation in Germany and Italy* (Minneapolis: Augsburg, 1971), 37.

23. Cited in Bainton, *Here I Stand*, 292.

24. Quoted in Bainton, *Women of the Reformation*, 37.

25. Quoted in Smith, *Life and Letters of Martin Luther*, 179.

26. See Treu, "Katharina von Bora," 172.

27. Martin Brecht, *Martin Luther: Shaping and Defining the Reformation, 1521–1532*, trans. James L. Schaaf (Minneapolis: Fortress, 1990), 205.

28. Ibid., 206.

29. Quoted in Markwald and Markwald, *Katharina von Bora*, 147.

30. Ibid., 111.

31. Quoted in Charles Frederick Ledderhose, *The Life of Philip Melanchthon* trans. G. F. Krotel (Philadelphia: Lindsay & Blakiston, 1857), 323.

32. See Susan C. Karant-Nunn and Merry E. Wiesner-Hanks, eds., *Luther on Women* (New York: Cambridge University Press, 2003), 193.

33. Quoted in Moritz Meurer, *The Life of Martin Luther: Related from Original Authorities* (New York: Ludwig, 1848), 642.

34. J. H. Alexander, *The Ladies of the Reformation* (London: Westminster Discount Books, 1996), 212.

35. See Matt Carver, "The 'Klette' Hymns and the 'Klette' Quote," *Hymnoglypt*, May 1, 2010, http://matthaeusglyptes.blogspot.com/2010/05/klette-hymns-and-klette-quote .html (accessed December 1, 2016).

36. See ibid.

37. Anne Elizabeth Baker, *Glossary of Northamptonshire Words and Phrases*, vol. 1 (London: Smith, 1854), 90.

38. Cited in James Anderson, *Ladies of the Reformation* (London: Blackie, 1857), 75.

Chapter 12: "No Words Can Express My Heartbreak"

1. Cited in Diane Severance, "Albrecht Dürer, Reformation Media Man," *Christianity. com*, www.christianity.com/church/church-history/timeline/1201-1500/albrecht-drer -reformation-media-man-11629888.html (accessed December 1, 2016).

2. Heiko Oberman, *Luther: Man Between God and the Devil*, trans. Eileen Walliser-Schwarzbart (New Haven, CT: Yale University Press, 2006), 5.

3. Quoted in Roland H. Bainton, *Women of the Reformation in Germany and Italy* (Minneapolis: Augsburg, 1971), 40.

4. Ibid.

5. Oberman, *Luther*, 5.

6. Charles H. H. Wright, *A Protestant Dictionary* (London: Hodder and Stoughton, 1904), 385.

7. Dr. Volkmar Joestel, "Luther's Death," www.luther.de/en/jlt.html (accessed December 1, 2016).

8. Quoted in Ernst Kroker, *The Mother of the Reformation: The Amazing Life and Story of Katharine Luther*, trans. Mark E. DeGarmeaux (St. Louis, MO: Concordia, 2013), 221.

9. Quoted in Oberman, *Luther*, 8.

10. "Did Luther Recant on His Deathbed," *Beggars All: Reformation & Apologetics*, comment by Churchmouse, January 12, 2007, http://beggarsallreformation.blogspot .com/2007/01/did-luther-recant-on-his-deathbed.html (accessed on December 1, 2016).

11. Quoted in Rebecca Larson, "Katharina von Bora: A Married Nun," *Tudors Dynasty*, September 3, 2016, www.tudorsdynasty.com/katharina-von-bora-a-married-nun (accessed December 1, 2016).

12. Scott H. Hendrix, *Martin Luther: Visionary Reformer* (New Haven, CT: Yale University Press, 2015), 286.

13. Erwin Weber, "500th Anniversary of Katharina von Bora," *Lutheran Journal* 68.2 (1999), http://helios.augustana.edu/~ew/des/illustrated-articles/su53.html (accessed December 1, 2016).

14. See Rudolf K. Markwald and Marilynn Morris Markwald, *Katharina von Bora: A Reformation Life* (St. Louis, MO: Concordia, 2002), 181.

15. Kroker, *Mother of the Reformation*, 230–31.

16. See Bainton, *Women of the Reformation*, 40.

17. Hendrix, *Martin Luther*, 286.

18. Bainton, *Women of the Reformation*, 41.

19. Hendrix, *Martin Luther*, 287.

20. See Bainton, *Women of the Reformation*, 42.

21. Martin Treu, "Katharina von Bora, the Woman at Luther's Side," *Lutheran Quarterly* 13 (summer 1999): 173, www.lutheranquarterly.com/uploads/7/4/0/1/7401289/treu _katharina_von_bora.pdf (accessed December 1, 2016).

22. See Bainton, *Women of the Reformation*, 42.

23. See Treu, "Katharina von Bora," 173.

24. Quoted in Markwald and Markwald, *Katharina von Bora*, 193.

25. See Sandy Bardsley, *Venomous Tongues: Speech and Gender in Late Medieval England* (Philadelphia: University of Pennsylvania Press, 2006), 185 (note 23).

26. See "The Fountain of Youth by Lucas Cranach the Elder," *My Daily Art Display*, May 5, 2012, https://mydailyartdisplay.wordpress.com/2012/05/05/the-fountain-of -youth-by-lucas-cranach-the-elder (accessed December 1, 2016).
27. The entire poem remains under copyright but is made publicly available at poets.org (with copyright holder's permission), www.poets.org/poetsorg/poem/do-not-go-gentle -good-night (accessed December 1, 2016).

Epilogue: Brand Bora

1. Martin Treu, "Katharina von Bora, the Woman at Luther's Side," *Lutheran Quarterly* 13 (summer 1999): 157, www.lutheranquarterly.com/uploads/7/4/0/1/7401289/treu _katharina_von_bora.pdf (accessed December 1, 2016).
2. Andrew Pettegree, *Brand Luther: 1517, Printing, and the Making of the Reformation* (New York: Penguin, 2015), 279.
3. Ibid.

Index